Object Databases

THE ESSENTIALS

Mary E. S. Loomis, Ph.D.

ADDISON-WESLEY PUBLISHING COMPANY

Reading, Massachusetts • Menlo Park, California • New York
Don Mills, Ontario • Wokingham, England • Amsterdam • Bonn
Sydney • Singapore • Tokyo • Madrid • San Juan
Paris • Seoul • Milan • Mexico City • Taipei

Many of the designations used by manufacturers and sellers to distinguish their products are claimed as trademarks. Where those designations appear in this book and Addison-Wesley was aware of a trademark claim, the designations have been printed in initial caps or all caps.

The publisher offers discounts on this book when ordered in quantity for special sales. For more information please contact:

Corporate & Professional Publishing Group
Addison-Wesley Publishing Company
One Jacob Way
Reading, Massachusetts   01867

Loomis, Mary E. S.
    Object databases : the essentials / Mary E.S. Loomis.
        p.   cm.
    Includes bibliographical references and index.
    ISBN 0-201-56341-X (acid-free paper)
    1. Object-oriented databases.   I. Title.
QA76.9.D3L69   1995   94-26970
005.75—dc20   CIP

Text printed on recycled and acid-free paper.
1 2 3 4 5 6 7 8 9 10   CRW   97969594
First Printing, October 1994

*To my colleagues from the early days of
the ODMG: Tom Atwood, Rick Cattell,
Joshua Duhl, Guy Ferran, Jacob Stein
and Drew Wade.*

CONTENTS

PREFACE

Object technology is one of the hottest topics in the software industry, and object database management is a key aspect of this technology. This book is about the essential aspects of object databases. It will help you better understand how object databases fit into the spectrum of technology offerings. It will prepare you to determine whether relational databases or object databases are more appropriate for your applications, and will give you fundamental information necessary to the evaluation of commercial object database management systems. The book does not contain details about particular products, because that information is so quickly dated. Instead, the emphasis is on providing material that will give you a broad base of understanding about the technology.

There is some confusion in the industry about exactly what an object database is. This confusion is understandable when you consider the loose way that we use hot adjectives like "object" and "object-oriented." *Object Databases: The Essentials* is about databases that are closely coupled with one or more object programming languages, usually C++ and/or Smalltalk. It is not about extended relational databases, which provide some object-oriented capabilities in the context of the relational database model. While extended relational databases are important, they are not the topic of focus here.

The book assumes only minimal previous knowledge about object technology in general, object programming, or database management. However, it is also intended to be valuable for readers with extensive backgrounds and experience in these areas. Much of the tutorial material about object principles, database principles, and relational databases has been isolated into easily identified sections of the text. There are a few examples that use code, mostly C++ and SQL, but I have endeavored not to get caught up in the details of syntax and interfaces.

The book starts with a chapter that explains the role of object database management systems (object DBMSs). It provides a "big-picture" perspective on the technology and discusses the fundamental reasons for use of object databases. The next several chapters give a balanced treatment of the programming language and database perspectives of object databases. Object databases in many ways represent the marriage of object programming and database management technologies. Depending on which of these technologies is more dominant in a developer's or vendor's perspective, different aspects of object databases become more important than others. Chapter 2 discusses object databases from a programming language perspective. You will learn what object programmers typically expect from object databases. Chapter 3 discusses object databases from a database management perspective. Here you will see the other point of view: What database people typically expect from object databases. Chapter 4 then confronts the technical areas where the object database and programming perspectives clash. Understanding these clash areas will help you better understand the differences between the commercial object DBMS products, which are largely due to their vendors' positions in the object programming/database management technology space.

Chapter 5 discusses an alternative to object databases: Using a relational DBMS with an object programming language. This chapter will be useful both for programmers who may not be familiar with relational DBMSs but who are trying to determine whether an object or relational database is more appropriate for their needs, and for relational database users who are trying to understand the differences and similarities between object and relational database technologies. The chapter shows what has to be done to make a relational database appear to contain objects, an illusion that is necessary to enable an object programming language like C++ or Smalltalk to access or store data in relational tables.

Chapters 6 through 9 are somewhat more technical than the other chapters. Chapter 6 discusses a fundamental aspect of object databases: Support for an object model. The object model presented here is that of the Object Database Management Group (ODMG), a consortium of the object DBMS vendors and other companies who are dedicated to the establishment and broad acceptance of important object database standards. Chapter 7 goes into some detail about how object DBMSs store and find objects. It discusses several aspects of the architectures of object DBMSs: Their process structures, their relationship to virtual memory, and their client-server configurations. It also discusses various ways that object DBMSs achieve their performance characteristics: Addressing techniques, caching, clustering, indexing, and replication. Chapter 8 focuses on object sharing, another fundamental aspect of object databases. It discusses locking, logging, transaction management, and versioning. Chapter 9 is about querying objects, an often misunderstood aspect of object databases. The chapter focuses on the need for expressing queries in a variety of styles. For example, the query requirements of C++, Smalltalk, and SQL programmers are quite different.

Chapters 10 and 11 are more oriented toward products and markets. Chapter 10 is about evaluating object DBMSs. It does not give details about particular products; for these you should consult the vendors or other books. Rather, it discusses the criteria you should consider in evaluating object DBMS products. The chapter emphasizes benchmarking and performance. Chapter 11 contains my opinions about the future direction of the object DBMS market. Mostly it discusses what I think are the major challenges that must be met by the object DBMS vendors in order for the object database market to continue to grow.

The references have been collected at the end of the book, rather than in each chapter. This is because some references would have appeared repeatedly. There is also what I hope you'll find to be a useful and comprehensive index.

ACKNOWLEDGMENTS

I want first to acknowledge the countless hours of conversation and discussion I've enjoyed over the years with Tom Atwood, who more than anyone else has helped me to understand this technology. I have also gained much understanding from many other colleagues, notably Rick Cattell, Kee Ong, Drew Wade, Guy Ferran, and Joshua Duhl. The book has benefited substantially from the thoughtful comments of the reviewers: Rick Cattell, Dave Jordan, Richard Helm, Jeff Poulin, and Peter DeVries. Thanks are also due to the numerous attendees at presentations I have given at various object- and database-related conferences who persevered through early versions of this material and contributed to my understanding of the importance of the fundamentals.

I want to give special thanks to Rick Friedman and his colleagues at SIGS, who through the *Journal of Object-Oriented Programming* provided me a venue for exploration of many of the ideas published here. Their encouragement and deadlines have kept me writing when many other pastimes have beckoned.

Special thanks go to Allison and Eleanor, who provided much welcomed incentive, encouragement, and diversion.

M.E.S.L.

CHAPTER 1

The Role of Object DBMSs

EXPECTATIONS FOR OBJECT TECHNOLOGY ARE HIGH

Object technology is of great interest in the software world, perhaps because it promises to help solve real problems. Expectations generally cited for object technology include

- improved software quality, reliability, testability, and extensibility

- shorter development times

- increased programmer productivity

- greater reusability of code; see, for example, [Gart92], [IDC92], [ITG93].

Managers and programmers alike expect easier application maintenance and improved ability to deal more effectively with increasingly complex applications. These applications may be media-rich (e.g., incorporating voice, video, image, and text) and involve interactions among groups of users. They may be sensitive to the context in which they're used and may present information and functionality in ways that are customized to users' preferences.

Why do these benefits accrue from using object technology? One reason is that code developed using object design techniques and implemented with an object programming language tends to be well modularized. This modularization helps localize the effects of changes and results in manageable, relatively small, source-code building blocks. These software blocks, or objects, can be composed to combine functionality and specialized to deliver new functionality (see Fig. 1-1). Groups of objects can be managed as domain-specific frameworks tailored to the needs of particular application areas. One of the few difficulties introduced by this extensive modular-

1

FIGURE 1-1.
USING OBJECTS TO BUILD APPLICATIONS.

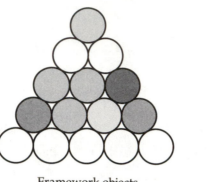 

Framework objects

Assembled, customized
application

ization is analyzing interactions between blocks, especially on a system-wide scale.

Developers expect improved productivity because object technology provides a modeling approach that is relatively unconstrained by software implementation techniques. The result is that objects help reduce the conceptual gap that a designer has to deal with in tackling a real-world problem domain. Developers also expect object programs to be easier to maintain, modify, and extend than programs written with conventional techniques. This flexibility should allow software developers to respond more rapidly to changes in and new requirements. Object programming languages and environments tend to encourage an incremental approach to software development and facilitate building reusable software components.

The promise of these benefits is tantalizing. People expect object technology to obliterate some of the following common complaints about the software business:

- Software is buggy, and it doesn't do what I want it to do.

- It takes too long to get those guys to deliver the software I need, and by the time they give me something, my needs have changed and the software is nearly worthless.

- Why does it seem like software development is still approached in a custom-craftsman way? Every time we write an application, we seem to start over from scratch. I'm tired of writing the same old drivers and routines over and over.

The evidence is still primarily anecdotal (see [Harm93] and [Love93]), but it indicates that object technology really does provide value to meet the expectations previously cited. A major reason for the benefits of object technology is the synergy achieved by using a consistent approach in all the various aspects of software development.

Let's now consider more precisely what this consistent approach of object technology is, and then we'll focus on object databases.

AN OBJECT IS A SOFTWARE BUILDING BLOCK

Many kinds of products today are labeled "object-oriented." The principles of object technology (see the sidebar on basic object technology principles) apply across all aspects of software development. Object technology can be used to construct nearly any kind of software, and many kinds of software can exhibit characteristics of object technology.

SIDEBAR: BASIC OBJECT TECHNOLOGY PRINCIPLES

The principles of object technology apply to all aspects of software development: methodologies, analysis and design tools, user interfaces, programming languages, databases, and operating systems. The common terminology and basic principles [Loom92c] are as follows:

- **Modularization**—Develop and write software in small, understandable modules of data structures and operations allowable on those data. These modules are known as *objects.*

- **Encapsulation**—Distinguish clearly between the interfaces of an object, which describe *what* the object does, and the implementation of that object, which defines *how* it does what it does.

- **Typing**—Group together all objects that have the same interfaces, that is, the same characteristics, and treat them as being of the same type.

- **Inheritance**—Reuse what you've already done, defining new types that have all the characteristics of an already-defined type, plus some additional characteristics. The new, derived type inherits the shared characteristics from the already-defined type.

- **Messaging**—Ask an object to perform one of its functions by sending it a message, phrased in a simple, standardized way, independent of how or where the object is implemented.

- **Polymorphism**—Use meaningful names for operations. The system will figure out at runtime exactly which operation code to invoke, based on the type of object that receives the message. *Polymorphism* is the ability of different kinds of objects to respond to the same message. The same operation name, such as `get_age, display,` or `get_YTD_compensation,` can have quite different actions, depending on whether the receiving object is a person or time-series data, a photo image or a bar chart, an hourly employee or a salesperson, and so forth. Message overloading and dynamic binding make polymorphism possible.

An object is a software building block. Object technology involves designing and implementing software in well-defined modular components, which interact with each other to provide some desired functionality. Each component has a data structure and performs a set of actions or operations, whose implementation need not be known by any other requesting component. Components need to be aware only of each other's interfaces. An object model provides a representation of real-world entities, with their behavior and interactions. For example, an object model of a computer system may include a variety of objects: printers, servers, accounts, users, network connections, desktop machines, and so forth. An object model of a business may include employees, customers, accounts, products, vendors, orders, warehouses, departments, and so forth.

An ideally architectured object environment would enable objects to use each other's services, even if their developers did not collaborate. Software interoperability in heterogeneous, distributed computing environments is the objective of standards like the Common Object Request Broker

Architecture (CORBA) from the Object Management Group (OMG) [Sole92]. CORBA includes the Interface Definition Language (IDL) for specifying object interfaces, a repository making those specifications available, and message-brokering services to deliver interobject requests. The intent is to enable developers to combine objects in unforeseen ways to meet their requirements. This kind of flexibility is currently available primarily within single-vendor product families such as Microsoft Office, which, for example, enables presentation objects to be incorporated in document objects.

OBJECTS ARE EVERYWHERE

Because the various aspects of software can share an object model foundation and can be built on the same basic principles, the synergy across the software disciplines using object technology can be stronger than previously possible. The technical areas overlap and together comprise a complete object solution set (see Fig. 1-2).

An object methodology provides process and models that promote an object approach to analysis, design, and implementation. There are numerous published methodologies and modeling techniques, for example, [Booc91], [Cole94], [Jaco92], [Mart92], [Rumb91], [Shla88], and [Wirf90]. Many of these have been compared in available literature, including

FIGURE 1-2.
OBJECT SOLUTIONS INVOLVE MULTIPLE, OVERLAPPING TECHNOLOGIES.

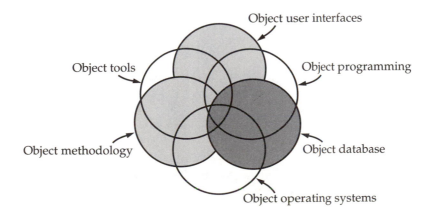

Object user interfaces
Object tools
Object programming
Object methodology
Object database
Object operating systems

[Crib92] and [OMG92]. Some approaches extend and integrate data models (e.g., entity–relationship models), process models (like hierarchic structure diagrams or data-flow diagrams), and state models (such as state transition diagrams and Petri models). Others introduce entirely new notational schemes.

Object tools support the techniques of the object methodologies. They provide object-oriented software engineering environments, from two points of view: being object-oriented themselves and constructing object-oriented applications. There are tools for all aspects of the software development process, ranging from object requirements analysis through systems design to class library and object database design, object program design, and generation of code, libraries, and database schemas. Tools are becoming available to support debugging, testing, integration, system testing, code versioning and control, document generation, and maintenance of object code.

A *graphical user interface* (GUI) is commonly considered to be an object-oriented user interface system. An object-oriented user interface ideally provides an extensible set of user-interaction capabilities, built on a model of well-defined operations that are invoked in particular contexts. Such an interface is typically graphical and can be used to display a broad range of data types: character, image, voice, and so forth. Perhaps the most familiar example of a GUI is found on every Macintosh or Windows system. These systems link data with the operations that can be executed on that data. For example, opening a file is done in the context of the application that created that file and makes that application's operations immediately available on the file.

An *object programming language* enables a programmer to develop code using the principles of object technology. An object programming language is used to code modules (i.e., objects) that interact with each other via message protocols. The language environment sometimes includes code for a class library of modules, which are extensible and refinable by programmers. These libraries can provide useful starting points for many applications. They may contain low-level reusable components providing basic data structures (e.g., date, array, queue, list) and algorithms. The most widely used object programming languages today are C++ and Smalltalk.

OOCOBOL, also on the market, provides an upwardly compatible path for COBOL programmers [Topp94]. Other object programming languages include Eiffel, Objective-C, CLOS, Actor, and Object Pascal.

An *object database management system* (DBMS) provides persistence for objects rather than for tables or records. It is well suited to support multi-user applications developed with an object programming language, where the users need to share data. The rest of this book is about object DBMSs.

An *object operating system* uses a model of objects instead of basing its operations on a variety of other artifacts. The resource manager manages objects, instead of separately managing files, users, memory, and so forth. The scheduler and dispatcher manage message traffic instead of queues of commands. The interrupt or event handler monitors the status of objects, handles exceptions, and understands a broad, extensible base of events. Object operating systems are products of NeXT, Taligent, and other companies.

OBJECTS BLUR INTERDISCIPLINARY BOUNDARIES

The object disciplines share common principles; in some sense they overlap, and the boundaries between them may blur. For example, in the past, DBMSs and programming languages were quite separate. Relational DBMSs use SQL—a language specifically designed to define and manipulate tables—and SQL is embedded in a variety of programming languages, such as COBOL and C. In contrast, an object DBMS uses an object programming language as its database language, rather than introducing a separate database interface. An object DBMS that supports C++ uses C++ as the data definition and manipulation language. Likewise, an object DBMS that supports Smalltalk uses Smalltalk as the data definition and manipulation language. Some object DBMSs are multilingual and support both C++ and Smalltalk.

Similarly, the boundary between database manager and operating system can blur with object technology. An object operating system's object identification, location, and distribution facilities provide basically the same functionality as these facilities from an object DBMS. An object operating system's persistence mechanism, traditionally referred to as the file system, might actually be provided by embedding an object DBMS in the operating system. The blurring between product categories can at first be quite confusing, but over time it should simplify the application development process.

CLASSICAL SOFTWARE DEVELOPMENT IS A VAULTING PROCESS

Figure 1-3 illustrates a view of the typical software development process. There are several quite separate activities, with high walls between them. Consider these three: analysis and design, programming, and database work. In large organizations the people who work in these areas can be in essentially different worlds. They use different terminology, different tools, and have very different perspectives from each other. These differences erect barriers in the software development process. Dealing with these barriers might be called the "vaulting approach" to software development [Loom90b].

Analysis and design activities use a variety of conceptual models: entity–relationship diagrams, structured analysis and design charts, dataflow diagrams, and so forth. These models attempt to represent more-or-

FIGURE 1-3.
THE VAULTING APPROACH TO SOFTWARE DEVELOPMENT.

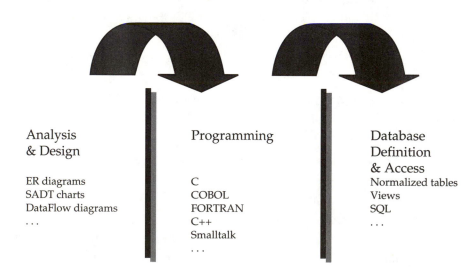

Analysis
& Design

ER diagrams
SADT charts
DataFlow diagrams
. . .

Programming

C
COBOL
FORTRAN
C++
Smalltalk
. . .

Database
Definition
& Access

Normalized tables
Views
SQL
. . .

less formally some aspect of the real world and how a problem is to be solved using the capabilities of the computer environment.

Programming is accomplished with a variety of languages, each with its own expression techniques and models of how to express operations and define and manipulate data. Note that these models are quite different from the models of the analysis and design techniques. Programming is still in part the art of expressing analysis and design models in statements that a compiler or interpreter can accept. This process can be arduous and difficult, especially if the developers of the design specifications have vanished or are otherwise unavailable.

Database definition and access introduce additional transformations. The database languages and models have traditionally been significantly different from the programming languages and models. DBMSs have their own languages and models. For example, many people built their careers as IMS experts, becoming proficient in the intricacies of the very specialized and arcane interfaces of the IMS DBMS product. More recently, another generation has learned the details of the relational model and become highly skilled in SQL, the standard language for relational DBMS products.

Programming and database work have inherently different perspectives. Embedding SQL in programming languages immediately shows some of these differences. For example, programming languages like C and COBOL are record-at-a-time languages, while SQL is a set-at-a-time language (see Fig. 1-4). SQL operates on and produces tables. SQL cursors are the mechanism relational DBMSs introduced as a way to deliver the table elements one at a time to the programming environment. Cursor manipulation is one of the more difficult aspects of working with a relational DBMS. This mechanism for penetrating the model-mismatch barrier between the programming language and DBMS has been a source of many bugs and maintenance headaches.

VAULTING INTRODUCES WORK AND ERRORS

Each time the software development process requires "vaulting" the walls between disciplines, there are significant barriers to overcome. One kind of model must be translated to another type of model. One set of terminology and language styles needs to be interfaced with another set, and

FIGURE 1-4.
EMBEDDING SET-ORIENTED SQL IN RECORD-ORIENTED C.

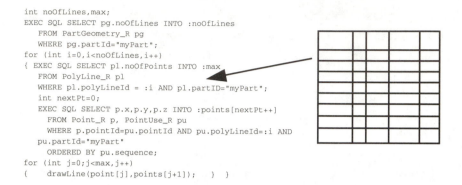

```
int noOfLines,max;
EXEC SQL SELECT pg.noOfLines INTO :noOfLines
    FROM PartGeometry_R pg
    WHERE pg.partId="myPart";
for (int i=0,i<noOfLines,i++)
{ EXEC SQL SELECT pl.noOfPoints INTO :max
    FROM PolyLine_R pl
    WHERE pl.polyLineId = :i AND pl.partID="myPart";
    int nextPt=0;
    EXEC SQL SELECT p.x,p.y,p.z INTO :points[nextPt++]
      FROM Point_R p, PointUse_R pu
      WHERE p.pointId=pu.pointId AND pu.polyLineId=:i AND
    pu.partId="myPart"
      ORDERED BY pu.sequence;
for (int j=0;j<max,j++)
{    drawLine(point[j],points[j+1]);    }  }
```

the development issue is tackled from a significantly different viewpoint. The transformations between disciplines can be problematic. Vaulting each of these walls has undesirable effects and can impede progress toward the overall goal of quickly delivering effective, efficient, and economical software to users. Each set of transformations requires work, consumes resources, and introduces a nontrivial potential for errors. Each transformed representation is a step farther from the real-world problem that the software is intended to solve. The coupling of this vaulting approach with the standard long-term waterfall model of the software development lifecycle (see Fig. 1-5) has led to a software crisis now widely recognized throughout the industry.

CASE TRIES TO ADDRESS THE SOFTWARE PROBLEM

The computer-aided software engineering (CASE) industry had the potential to bring some relief to this software problem by providing development teams with a variety of tools, each tailored to a particular aspect of analysis, design, and implementation. Unfortunately for many hopeful customers and investors, this form of CASE did not work very well. By the early 1990s, labeling a product "CASE" was not necessarily attractive. CASE gained connotations of being unwieldy, unrealistic, and ill suited for the ever-more-popular local-area network (LAN) and workgroup computing environments. There were numerous discussions at conferences like

FIGURE 1-5.
A CLASSIC WATERFALL MODEL OF SOFTWARE DEVELOPMENT.

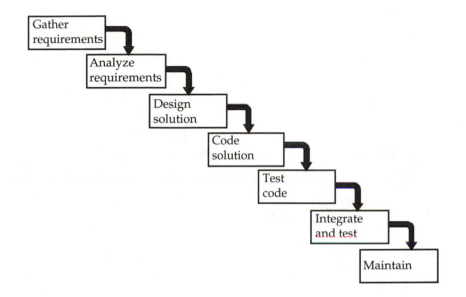

Software World and CASE World where the issue boiled down to "is CASE dead?" It proved difficult to plug together tools from multiple sources, even from within the same vendor, and the output of a tool used at one step of the process only rarely could be used as input by a tool at the next step.

Objects are now considered the "technology *du jour*," competing with "client–server" for label space. In 1992 and 1993 there were many debates about whether object technology was an alternative to CASE. There were panels at professional conferences pitting industry luminaries vehemently on either side of the issue. Some argued that object technology made CASE irrelevant; others claimed that objects would be the salvation of CASE; and a few exclaimed that objects were a fad. In fact, there is nothing inconsistent about object-CASE. Tools for object modeling, browsing class libraries, reusing code modules, linking with legacy databases, reengineering legacy code, customizing graphical user interfaces, and so forth are important to the viability of object technology for production environments. They are also important to the long-run viability of CASE. Several CASE vendors now feature object techniques in their toolkits.

OBJECT TECHNOLOGY TEARS DOWN THE WALLS

An alternative to the vaulting approach is to remove the walls. So far, the only technology that seems to make this feasible is object technology. The promise of object technology comes in large part from the use of a single, unified conceptual model—the object model—that can drive all aspects of development, from early conceptualization through maintenance.

Two important results of the no-vault approach (Fig. 1-6) are as follows:

- Improved productivity, because the vaulting activities are eliminated. For example, programming-language record-at-a-time statements don't have to be interfaced with the relational DBMS set-at-a-time model of operation. An object programming language's operations on collections of objects don't have to be interfaced with the relational model either. Both the object programming language and the object DBMS operate at the object level. In many cases, the code required to translate between the programming language model and the database model can essentially be eliminated. The result is fewer lines of code to design, write, and maintain.

- Better quality, because the opportunities for error introduced by the vaulting activities are avoided. Fewer lines of code typically means simpler code, and simpler code typically means fewer bugs.

The object models developed in analysis and design become not only the basis for the programming language's object model, but also for the database model. Only minimal tuning of the structure is required, and the entity cohesiveness and logical relationships among objects are used in implementing the physical database.

SIDEBAR: WHY OBJECT DATABASES?

Application developers decide to use object databases for the following reasons:

- They have decided to use object technology and they consider object databases to be part of that decision.

FIGURE 1-6.
THE NO-VAULT APPROACH TO SOFTWARE DEVELOPMENT.

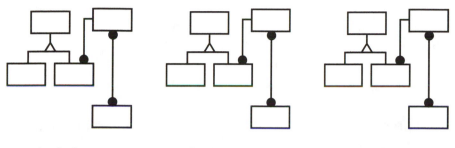

Analysis   Programming   Database
& Design   Definition
                                        & Access

- They have database applications, whose complexity is not handled well by the relational model.

- They have distributed applications, which can benefit by the distributed features and collaborative workgroup functionality of object databases.

The motivations that lead any particular project team to use an object database may not fall neatly into one of these three categories. However, these reasons are typical.

OBJECT DATABASES ARE INTEGRAL TO OBJECT TECHNOLOGY

Developers can tear down the wall between programming and database technologies by using an object DBMS with their object programming language. Application developers who have decided to use an object programming language often later decide to use an object DBMS because it fits well with the programming environment. Many of these developers also decide to use an object-oriented analysis and design methodology. They expect the combination of object-oriented analysis and design, object programming language, and object database to offer the benefits of a synergistic development environment. Design tools that generate class library code and object database schemas are also attractive to these developers.

Developers who first select an object programming language and then decide to use an object DBMS are typically building new applications with new databases. An object database becomes their primary source of object persistence. If applications require access to data in a legacy of relational databases, the developers may either build methods to access those systems directly or use gateway products, which provide C++ or Smalltalk interfaces to relational DBMSs. These gateways hide some of the intermodel transformation complexity from programmers.

OBJECT DATABASES SUPPORT COMPLEX APPLICATIONS

Other developers who use object DBMSs are motivated by the desire to satisfy the requirements of complex database applications, rather than by the desire to complement an object programming language. These applications generally involve highly interrelated data (e.g., product definitions, time series, bills of materials) and/or data that is not easily accommodated by the built-in relational data types (e.g., images, multimedia, text, documents). Some developers turn to an object DBMS after using a relational DBMS on their applications and finding that either the performance is unsatisfactory or the relational model is too confining. These people sometimes make statements like, "Our data is inherently object-oriented," or "We couldn't have done this without an object database."

These application developers make a database-driven decision to use an object database, and then find that they are also making an object technology-driven decision. Because of the range of programming languages that object DBMSs support, deciding to use an object database implies using object programming as well. This requirement will change as the marketplace evolves to offer additional object database application development tools, including object 4GLs, object report writers, and so forth.

OBJECT DATABASES SUPPORT DISTRIBUTED APPLICATIONS

A third reason that developers use an object DBMS is to support inherently distributed applications, in either local- or wide-area network environments. A "classic" example is in engineering information management. Here the object database functions as a repository of design data. The actual designs may be developed using computer-aided design (CAD) packages with their own proprietary, highly-tuned file systems or high-performance single-user persistent object storage managers, but the flow of design data between personal and group databases, the versioning of designs, and the cataloging of design information are managed by an object DBMS.

IN CLOSING . . .

The fundamental role of an object DBMS is to provide persistent storage management for objects in a way that

1. allows for highly efficient but easy access from object programming languages,

2. hides the complexities of distribution of objects across network sites, and

3. allows multiple users and applications shared, protected access to the objects.

The primary responsibility of object databases, as described in [Love93], is to provide "pickled objects"—enabling objects to be preserved so that they will last longer than if they were just created by an object programming language and allowed to disappear along with other program variables when the program ended execution. An object should be viewed as data *plus* behavior. Coupling them in an object database means that persistence of data structures is no longer a separate issue from management of the code. Commercial object DBMSs support a range of functionality for pickling objects. This book is devoted to helping you understand the essentials of how object DBMSs fulfill their fundamental role.

CHAPTER 2

Object Databases from a Programming Language Perspective

One reason to use an object database is its synergy with object programming. Object DBMSs and object programming languages support a common object model. This shared system reduces the work required of programmers to design and code applications. However, programmers and database people sometimes have distinct viewpoints and expectations of object database technology. This chapter explores programmers' expectations; Chapter 3 will consider the database perspective.

SOME APPLICATIONS REQUIRE PERSISTENCE FOR OBJECTS

From the programming language point of view, a basic feature of an object database is *persistent object storage.* Some programmers even refer to an object DBMS as a persistent storage manager. The database provides a way to extend the lifetime of objects past the termination of the run unit that creates them. An object is persistent if it is created by one program but can be accessed by another, even after the creating program has ended. A persistent object might be stored on a hard disk, a diskette, magnetic tape, or any other medium that does not lose its memory when the power is turned off.

A database allows objects to live longer. Persistence is especially important for applications constructed as sequences of programs and as programs that execute on multiple machines in a network. An object that is not persistent is said to be *transient* (see Fig. 2-1). A program can create many transient objects, none of which lives past that program's execution. An example of a simple transient object is a programming language variable. For example, the integer variable i is usable throughout the scope of its declaration, but it does not exist outside that scope. The variable i disappears when the program ends.

Programming languages provide several ways to scope the lifetimes of transient objects. For example, a transient object may be scoped for the lifetime of a procedure or for an entire process. The object ceases to exist when the procedure is exited or the process terminates. An object database provides a third lifetime alternative: a persistent object's space is allocated from physical storage managed by the object DBMS at runtime, and the object DBMS ensures that persistent objects continue to exist after process termination.

PROGRAMMERS WANT PERFORMANCE

An object database must provide persistence and be fast. Programmers basically expect that access to persistent objects will be as fast as access to transient objects. This is, of course, in general, impossible, because access to a persistent object may require accessing a disk and/or traversing a network. In fact, with virtual memory management on most operating systems, access to transient objects may force disk access anyway.

An object DBMS attempts to meet performance expectations in several ways:

FIGURE 2-1.
TRANSIENT AND PERSISTENT OBJECTS.

RAM *DISK*

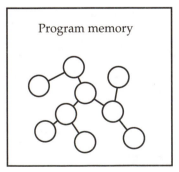 

Program memory Non-volatile storage

Transient objects Persistent objects

- One objective is to make the speed of access to persistent objects that have already been brought into main memory as close as possible to the speed of the programming language's access to main-memory objects. This is a performance parameter commonly measured in benchmarks that evaluate object DBMS products. Meeting this speed objective requires clever management of in-memory pointers and close interaction with the language at runtime.

- Second, an object DBMS tries to minimize network traffic by caching objects in the program memory space and by transferring aggregates of objects together in a single-server access, rather than transferring objects one at a time. The guiding principle is to transfer requested objects together without transferring too many additional objects. In some cases the best solution is to access objects individually.

- Third, an object DBMS tries to minimize disk traffic by wisely clustering objects on storage so that a single disk access acquires multiple objects that a program is going to need. Maintaining good physical clustering can be complicated when there is substantial update, delete, and insert activity; when patterns of access change; or when different programs have different clustering requirements for overlapping sets of objects.

The performance characteristics of an object DBMS are largely determined by the addressing scheme it uses and the distribution of objects on the persistent media. A programming language like C++ can simply use virtual memory addresses to locate transient objects. These memory addresses do not suffice for locating persistent objects. A program may need to access persistent objects that are stored on any of a large number of devices, located at multiple computers in a network.

THERE ARE SEVERAL SOURCES OF PERSISTENCE

There are several ways to make programming language objects persistent. A common technique is to use the file system directly. For example, a C++ programmer can use C++ language constructs and C++ libraries directly to write objects to files, where they become persistent. Using the file system for object persistence requires the programmer to write code that flattens the in-memory representation of objects to structures that can be stored in files.

Typically, the transformations between objects and flat-file representations are not trivial. For example, the logic may include relatively complicated code to traverse references between objects. These references are implemented as pointers and represented by memory addresses while the objects are transient and under C++ control. The code to write objects to files must provide some means other than pointers to represent references, since the memory addresses will not be valid when it is time to read the objects back in from the file structures. And this brings up the other half of the file system persistence solution: the programmer has to write code to read the saved data from the file structure back into objects (see Fig. 2-2). Further complications arise when developers change class specifications and thereby invalidate file structures. The mapping transformation code also must be adjusted appropriately.

Several options exist for storing objects persistently with sharability (see Fig. 2-3). For example, objects can be stored persistently in relational

FIGURE 2-2.
FILE SYSTEM PERSISTENCE REQUIRES TRANSFORMATIONS [Loom93b].

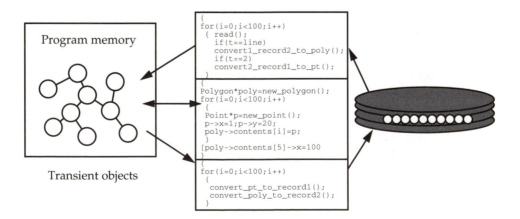

FIGURE 2-3.
SOURCES OF OBJECT PERSISTENCE WITH SHARABILITY.

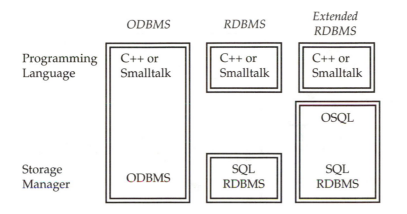

databases. This approach can be tempting in organizations that already use relational DBMSs for various applications. The relational database approach to object persistence is somewhat like the file system approach, but it can require even more transformation code. A relational DBMS imposes additional data representation constraints, which must be considered in the transformation logic. Writing this transformation logic is the same kind of work Chapter 1 refers to in the discussion of the vaulting approach to software development. Each transformation requires development and runtime resources and introduces nontrivial potential for errors. Not only must objects be flattened, but they must also be partitioned into record structures for storage in relational tables (see Fig. 2-4). The programmer must supply the logic for mapping objects into the formats required by SQL.

Another alternative is to use an extended-relational database for object persistence. The extended-relational DBMS products augment the relational table model to accommodate some aspects of objects. This approach has the advantage of burying some of the transformation mapping responsibilities into the DBMS itself, rather than leaving them all to the programmer. The transformation mapping is still necessary, however, because the underlying storage facility is still a relational database. A major concern regarding

FIGURE 2-4.
RELATIONAL DATABASE PERSISTENCE REQUIRES
TRANSFORMATIONS [Loom93b].

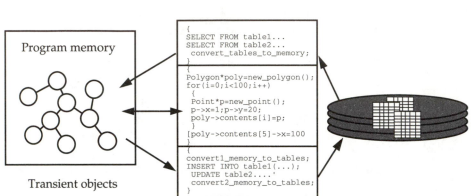

extended-relational DBMS products is how well they will perform when complex mappings are required between the application's object model and relational tables.

Objects can be stored persistently in an object database with no transformation code. The object database solution merges the notions of the in-memory and persistent storage models into a consistent, single-level store (see Fig. 2-5). Because the object DBMS and object programming language both use the same type system and object model, the programmer does not have to write any code to transform the in-memory representation into a structure the object DBMS can manage. Because the underlying storage facility also does not have to transform between models, performance can be excellent even for complex objects. Neither development nor runtime vaulting is required. And because the object DBMS is a DBMS, the objects are sharable.

PROGRAMMERS WANT INVISIBLE DATABASES

Many object programmers want persistence but do not want to deal with a DBMS that is separate from the programming environment. The programming language perspective imposes the requirement that in addition to being fast, *the object DBMS interface must be well integrated with the pro-*

FIGURE 2-5.
OBJECT DATABASES SUPPORT A SINGLE-LEVEL MEMORY MODEL.

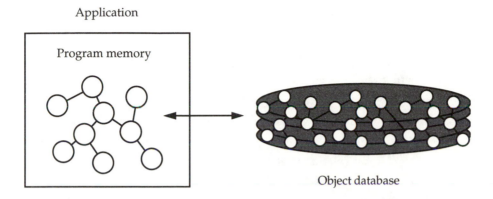

gramming language environment. Whether the object DBMS is well integrated or not is determined by whether

1. the object DBMS introduces its own data model or shares the programming language's type system, and

2. there is a simple mapping between transient and persistent objects.

The programmer would like to use the object DBMS as if it were part of the language. In fact, many programmers would prefer that the object database were simply invisible.

Object DBMS products address these two integration requirements by using the object programming language as the database interface language [Atwo91], [Banc90], [Catt91]. An object DBMS for C++ uses C++ for database access. This means that C++ is used to declare and manipulate not just transient objects, but also persistent objects. Similarly, an object DBMS for Smalltalk uses Smalltalk for database access. The programmer stays within the language's paradigm and does not have to switch models or modes of thinking or syntax when dealing with persistent objects. This is possible because the language environment and the object DBMS share the same type system. Any object structure that can be defined in the programming language can be stored directly in the object database. The programmer does not have to model objects using one model for the programming language and another for the database.

RELATIONAL DBMSs USE AN SQL INTERFACE

The integration of object databases and programming languages is in sharp contrast to the way that relational DBMSs work. A relational DBMS uses its own language—SQL [Melt93]—for all database operations, regardless of the programming language environment. If a relational DBMS is used to provide persistence for an object program, the application programmer must use one language, for example, C++ or Smalltalk, for transient objects and SQL for relational database access. SQL is quite different from C++; for instance, each has its own set of keywords.

SQL operands and their results are tables. SQL also defines the type system supported by a relational DBMS. These are the only types allowed in a relational database. The relational type system is not the same as the type system of any programming language, object-oriented or not. The relational type system includes tables and a set of predefined primitives (e.g., DECIMAL, INTEGER, CHARACTER). A relational DBMS's INTEGER type is not necessarily the same as a C++ int type. Interfacing the two introduces the need for type checking whenever data is passed across the boundary between the database and programming language. Flipping back and forth between C++ or Smalltalk and SQL is not easy for many programmers. SQL is not invisible when embedded in C++ or Smalltalk code.

SEAMLESS INTEGRATION HELPS IMPROVE PRODUCTIVITY

The integration of an object programming language and an object database enables all objects to be treated with a single syntax, as well as a unified model and type system. The object programmer therefore typically needs to write fewer lines of code to store and access objects in an object database than in a relational database, because relational DBMSs do not understand object models. They understand only tables and a built-in set of data types. Logic to handle other aspects of the object model, such as inheritance and relationships, must be built into relational application code.

The relational philosophy (and the view of all prior generations of data management technology) is that databases are special, external resources that are quite separate from programs and should not be in the domain of the programming environment. The programmers should just give commands using the database language SQL and the needed data will be delivered. But the programmer needs to know, in fact, *has* to know, when he or she is dealing with the database and when he or she is working in the programming language environment.

The object philosophy is quite different. An explicit objective of object DBMSs is to bring the programming environment and the persistence mechanism closer together. The programmer can deal with persistent and transient objects using not only the same model, but also the same syntax. The result is that the programmer need not be so conscious of which objects are transient and which are persistent. Chapter 5 includes examples of some of the differences between using an object database to store objects and using a relational database to store those same objects. In some cases, the differences in complexity and number of lines of code required are startling.

Thus, a major criterion that object programmers apply when evaluating and selecting an object DBMS product is how well the product fits into the programming environment. Unfortunately it is not as simple as just answering the question, "How seamless is the interface to the object DBMS?" It turns out that different programmers mean different things when they judge seamlessness. This is especially true in the C++ community. Next we'll discuss some reasons why.

SOME PROGRAMMERS WANT TO USE ONLY STANDARD C++

To some C++ programmers an object DBMS fits well with the C++ environment only if the object DBMS interface uses the syntax of the ANSI C++ standard. These programmers consider the most attractive object DBMSs to be those that introduce no syntax or preprocessors. These programmers want to use standard C++ for declaration of all classes and for manipulation of both transient and persistent objects.

An object DBMS that meets the needs of these programmers provides a class library as its C++ interface. A programmer invokes object DBMS functionality by invoking methods in this class library—for example, methods to connect to databases and to commit transactions. These object DBMSs can be used with a broad range of C++ compilers from systems vendors and other independent suppliers.

Although this "standard C++" approach faithfully uses the object programming language as the database language, it usually results in the database being far from invisible. The use of persistence appears explicitly in both the `.h` files that declare C++ classes, and the `.cxx` files that encode logic. For example, these object DBMSs typically introduce a class that provides persistent behavior. Any C++ class that is potentially going to have persistent instances must be derived from this base persistent class. These object DBMSs also typically supply templated types to be used for inter-object references instead of using C++ pointers. For example, the following C++ code declares that the variable `p` is to point to an object of the class `Professor`:

```
Professor *p;
```

If `Professor` were a class known to the object DBMS, then the following C++ code would be used to declare that the variable `p` is to refer to (which is logically the same as pointing to) an object of the class `Professor`:

```
Ref<Professor> p;
```

Both code fragments use standard C++.

Bringing this kind of persistence to an existing C++ application implies changing the source code of appropriate class definitions to include inheritance from the base persistence class and replacing pointers by appropriate reference types. Similarly, the application code must then use these reference types instead of pointers for references between persistent objects. Thus there is some work required to take existing C++ code and adapt it for use with an object database. The philosophy that rationalizes these changes is that thought really must be given to how to add persistence to an existing application. This philosophy stems partly from the database viewpoint that programs should treat persistent data differently than transient data. Note that this is not necessarily the programmer's viewpoint.

OTHER PROGRAMMERS WANT A CLEANER INTERFACE, EVEN IF THE C++ IS NONSTANDARD

In contrast, other C++ programmers judge seamlessness by how easy it is to take existing C++ code and use it with the object DBMS. An object database that appeals to these programmers goes farther toward becoming invisible. These programmers want incorporation of persistence to involve as few changes to their C++ code as possible. For instance, they would like an object DBMS for which all classes are persistence-capable, without introduction of a base persistent class. Additionally, they would like to be able to use C++ pointer syntax between objects, regardless of whether the objects are persistent or transient. They would prefer not to distinguish between the semantics and the syntax of relationship traversal paths and pointers.

Vendors of object DBMSs that provide this degree of integration with C++ sometimes supply their own C++-development environments, which preprocess C++ code to understand its use of persistence. For example, a preprocessor can detect pointers used for references between persistent objects and will handle them differently than pointers between transient objects. Preprocessors enable the object DBMS to introduce syntax that isn't really C++ but that is quite natural for the C++ programmer and may even be cleaner than the interfaces possible when standard C++ syntax is adhered to strictly.

DATABASE STANDARDS ARE APPEARING

Both these positions for interfacing an object DBMS with C++ are viable. The simplest evidence is the fact that products with both kinds of C++ integration sell well in the marketplace. Both approaches have been factored into the efforts of the object DBMS vendors to standardize their interfaces. Their results have been published [Catt94] and will be referred to here as ODMG-93. The base level of the ODMG-93 model assumes the use of preprocessors, since standard C++ compilers cannot handle the keywords that ODMG-93 adds. The C++ "future" binding of ODMG-93 proposes a higher degree of seamlessness by enabling pointer syntax to be used to implement relationship traversal paths. The underlying object DBMS then must correctly handle pointers across devices and nodes of the network.

SMALLTALK OBJECTS CAN BE FILED IN IMAGES

The situation with Smalltalk object persistence is somewhat different from C++, in that Smalltalk provides its own form of persistence as part of the language. Smalltalk includes a facility to file the *Image,* which contains all an application's objects at a point in time. The Image becomes a persistent store that can be recovered in the future. In effect, the Image is like an elementary object database. Filing an Image requires no transformation code; the transient objects are stored directly as persistent objects. Therefore this solution to the persistence problem is very good in terms of productivity: it requires essentially no new work. However, it does not provide for sharability, recovery, query, or any of the other database functionality an object DBMS provides.

SHARABILITY HELPS MAKE APPLICATIONS SCALABLE

In addition to providing persistent storage, high-performance access to complex objects, and seamless integration with object programming environments, an object DBMS provides *sharability* of objects. Sharability is important to make object applications scalable. A scalable application can support growing numbers of users and can move from single-node to networked computing environments.

Object programming projects commonly start as single-user endeavors. However, many of these projects, when successful, will grow and need multiuser capabilities. Increasingly, they will be deployed in distributed computing environments. For a variety of reasons, the persistent objects an application needs may be stored at multiple sites in a network. Additional sites may be required for purposes of high availability through replication, for performance by reducing network traffic, or simply due to spreading popularity of an application. An object application is scalable only if the objects it needs can be moved in the network and reallocated to different sites without affecting the application source code. An application should never break just because an object has been moved.

The database features of an object DBMS make objects sharable and protect objects against damages from interference of multiple concurrent users, whether they are accessing objects on a single server, multiple servers, or complex configurations of many workstations and servers with mixes of local and shared databases. Chapter 3 introduces the object DBMS functions of concurrency control, transaction management, schema management, recoverability, and access control.

These DBMS features are not available when an application uses a file system directly for persistent storage of objects. Developers of an object application that is written to get persistence directly from files, may find that the application cannot scale to meet the requirements of a growing user base. Using an object database is a strategy for avoiding this problem and helping ensure the long-term success of the application. It is important to consider DBMS functions in the criteria that are applied to evaluate sources of object persistence. They sometimes are unwittingly omitted when an evaluation considers only a single-user programming language perspective.

IN CLOSING . . .

In this chapter we've seen that object programmers basically expect an object database to provide persistent storage for their application objects. They typically evaluate and select object DBMS products based on how they measure up on two criteria:

1. performance
2. how well the object DBMS integrates into the object programming environment.

File systems, relational DBMSs, and extended-relational DBMSs are other candidate sources of object persistence. However, file systems do not support the scalability and sharing requirements of distributed, multiuser applications and leave the programmer with the burden of transforming objects into flattened records. Relational DBMSs provide object sharability but are not well integrated with object programming languages, also leaving the programmer with the object transformation problem. Extended-relational DBMSs support their own object models but are not well integrated with object programming languages and require the use of a variant of SQL. Object DBMSs provide the persistent storage alternative that meets both of the object programmer's evaluation criteria.

CHAPTER 3

Object Databases from a Database Management Perspective

Chapter 2 introduced object programmers' typical expectations of object databases. They commonly view object DBMS as a persistent storage mechanism and want an integrated, seamless interface to the object programming environment. Now let's take another perspective and see what database people generally expect from object databases. Database people tend to compare object DBMSs more directly with relational DBMSs.

DATABASE PEOPLE WANT OBJECT SEMANTICS

From the database management point of view, a paramount feature of an object DBMS is *support for an object model rather than a table-oriented model*. This difference has significant implications for both the kinds of data that the database can store and the operations that the DBMS can perform.

Database people expect that one of the fundamental capabilities of an object DBMS is support for an object model. Because an object DBMS supports objects, object databases are not constrained to the tabular structures of the relational, set-oriented model. An object model is compared with the relational model in this chapter. If you are interested in more details of the relational model, see Chapter 5, which discusses using a relational DBMS to store objects.

OBJECT DBMSs SUPPORT AN EXTENSIBLE TYPE SYSTEM

One important characteristic of an object model is its extensible type system. Most object DBMS products ship with a built-in set of data types, and the application developer can define whatever additional types the application needs. For example, some applications need a `time-series` data type; others need an `address` type. The extensible type system gives the object database the ability to provide persistence for any kind of data that applications need. Applications are not required to translate objects from the programming language types to a set of built-in database types.

By contrast, a relational DBMS can support only tables and the fixed set of its built-in data types. An object DBMS can store any kind of data in an object database because it is not constrained to managing just tables or a particular set of built-in data types. The object DBMS can directly store any data types and structures that can be declared in the object programming environments it supports. The data type extensibility feature makes an object database a suitable source of sharable persistence for image, text, audio, video, and other media-rich kinds of data.

SIDEBAR: RELATIONAL DBMS PRINCIPLES

Relational DBMSs Support Tables with a Fixed Set of Data Types

All data stored in a relational database is modeled as if it were stored in tables. Each table is named and can have any number of columns and rows. Each column holds a particular type of data, and each row of values is conceptually like a record (see Fig. 3-1).

Each relational DBMS product supplies a fixed set of data types that can be used for columns. Only one type of data can be stored in any given column, and the programmer cannot extend the set of available data types. A relational DBMS that conforms to the SQL92 standard specification [ANSI92] supports the following data types:

```
CHARACTER and CHARACTER VARYING
BIT and BIT VARYING
NUMERIC
DECIMAL
INTEGER and SMALLINT
FLOAT
REAL
DOUBLE PRECISION
DATE
INTERVAL
TIME
TIMESTAMP
```

FIGURE 3-1.
BASIC RELATIONAL TABLE STRUCTURE AND TERMINOLOGY.

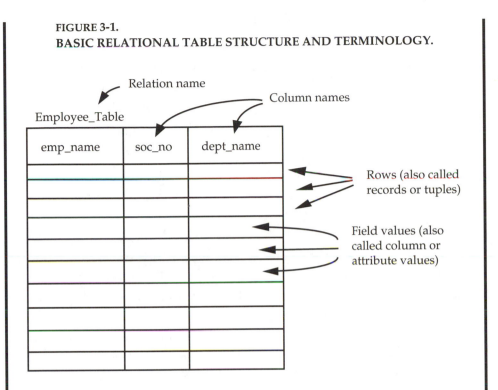

The list of built-in data types actually supported by many relational DBMS products is a subset of this list.

The table structures of a relational database are declared using the SQL **CREATE TABLE** statement. Each table is declared by specifying its name as well as the name and data type of each of its columns. For example:

```
CREATE TABLE Employee_Table
(soc_no         INTEGER,
 emp_name       CHARACTER VARYING,
 birth_date     DATE,
 dept_name      CHARACTER VARYING);
```

A relational DBMS enforces type checking on the built-in types when rows are inserted into database tables. For example, a relational DBMS will prevent an application from storing a character string in the soc_no or birth_date column. Some relational DBMSs also ensure the portability of these types across heterogeneous hardware platforms.

SQL is programming-language independent. Thus, a relational database defined using these built-in types can be accessed by multiple programming languages, say by both COBOL and C. The relational DBMS vendor provides type conversion routines in its embeddings of SQL in the various host programming languages. The ability to share data across programming languages is considered a major benefit of the relational DBMS approach.

Table Declarations Can Include Certain Constraints

The definition of a relational table can include certain constraints, which the relational DBMS can enforce at runtime. These constraint specifications capture additional semantics about the data, removing the need to implement that logic in applications.

One kind of constraint is a *uniqueness constraint,* which the table designer specifies by designating one or more columns of a table as its *primary key.* The values of these primary key columns uniquely identify the rows within the table. For example, the primary key of the example Employee_Table relation might be soc_no. The primary key of an Outstanding_Ordered_Item_Table relation might be the combination of invoice_no and line_item_no. No two rows in a table may have the same value for the primary key column(s). The table designer declares primary keys using the SQL PRIMARY KEY clause. For example:

```
CREATE TABLE Ordered_Item_Table
(invoice_no    CHARACTER(6),
 line_item_no  INTEGER,
 item_id       CHARACTER(7),
 item_qty      INTEGER,
 ...
 PRIMARY KEY (invoice_no, line_item_no)
 ...)
```

Intertable Relationships Are Represented by Common Values

The table designer uses the SQL FOREIGN KEY clause to designate that one or more columns represent an intertable relationship. The columns of a foreign key appear in some other table as a primary key. For example, `owner_no` might be designated as a foreign key in the `Account_Table` relation, with reference to the `Customer_Table` relation, where `customer_no` is the primary key:

```
CREATE TABLE Account_Table
     (account_no CHARACTER,
      owner_no INTEGER,
      PRIMARY KEY (account_no),
      FOREIGN KEY (owner_no)
           REFERENCES Customer_Table (customer_no);
```

The implication is that rows in `Account_Table` and `Customer_Table` are related by having matching values for `owner_no` and `customer_no`, respectively.

Referential Integrity Constraints Prevent "Dangling" References

The relational DBMS maintains the validity of these value-based relationships by ensuring that for each foreign key value, there is a matching primary key value in the appropriate table. Otherwise, the foreign key value references a nonexisting row and the relationship is bogus. This kind of constraint is called a *referential integrity constraint.*

Consider again the customer–account relationship. No `owner_no` value may exist in the `Account_Table` without there being a row in the `Customer_Table` with that same value for its `customer_no`. Violation of the referential integrity constraint could occur on insertion, deletion, or modification of data:

- An application could add an `Account_Table` row with a `customer_no` value that does not exist in the `Customer_Table`.

- An application could delete a `Customer_Table` row, leaving now-dangling rows with the no-longer-existing `customer_no` value in the `Account_Table`.

- An application could change the value of an `Account_Table` row's `customer_no` to a value that does not exist in the `Customer_Table`.

The table designer can use SQL to designate what action the DBMS should take to avoid violation of a referential integrity constraint. Such actions include CASCADE, SET NULL, SET DEFAULT, and NO ACTION. These can be specified as rules for the DBMS to apply ON UPDATE or ON DELETE. CASCADE means to trickle the update or delete from the table where the attribute was the primary key to the table where the attribute was the foreign key. Thus, when an application changes a primary key value, the DBMS will cascade the change to change the corresponding foreign key values as well. The other rules are self-evident; NO ACTION is the default.

The ability to specify referential integrity constraints has been in the SQL standard since 1989, but some relational DBMS products still do not enforce it.

Relational DBMSs Support Only Set Operations

Relational DBMSs support a set-based data model: relational databases are structured as sets, which are fixed-format tables whose row ordering is immaterial. A relational DBMS provides operators to access and manipulate these sets. The relational operators are based on mathematical set theory and are part of what is referred to as the "relational algebra." SQL, the most commonly used interface to relational databases, is built on the relational algebra. Understanding the fundamental operators that are the basis for SQL's manipulation capabilities is important for comparing relational DBMSs and object DBMSs. Three fundamental operators are restrict, project, and join.

The restrict operator applies a predicate to the elements of a set (i.e., the rows of a table), producing a set with only the qualifying elements. For example, using a fabricated but hopefully obvious syntax such as:

```
T1 := restrict Customer_Table [city_name = "Versailles"]
```

produces a set (i.e., table), named T1 containing the rows from the Customer_Table relation whose value for the city_name column is Versailles.

The project operator produces a table containing only specified columns of the argument table. For example:

```
T2 := project T1 [customer_no, city_name]
```

produces a table named `T2` containing all the `customer_no, city_name` pairs from the `T1` table.

The programmer could state the above `restrict` and `project` in SQL simply as:

```
T2 = SELECT customer_no, city_name
FROM Customer_Table
WHERE city_name = "Versailles";
```

The programmer specifies the restriction in the `WHERE` clause and the projection in the `SELECT` list.

The `join` operator combines two tables based on matching values of specified columns in each, producing a table with appropriately concatenated rows. For example:

```
T3 := join Customer_Table [customer_no] Invoice_Table
```

produces a table named `T3` containing rows created by combining the rows of the `Customer_Table` and `Invoice_Table` relations that have equal values for their `customer_no` columns.

The programmer could state this request in SQL simply as:

```
T3 = SELECT
FROM Customer_Table c, Invoice_Table i
WHERE c.customer_no = i.customer_no;
```

A request for the `customer_no, city_name, invoice_balance` triples for customers in the city of Versailles could be stated in SQL as:

```
T4 = SELECT c.customer_no, c.city_name, i.invoice_balance
FROM Customer_Table c, Invoice_Table i
WHERE c.city_name = "Versailles"
  AND c.customer_no = i.customer_no;
```

The programmer constructs complex `WHERE` clause predicates using boolean combinations (`AND, OR, NOT`) of simple predicates. For example:

```
T5 = SELECT c.customer_no, c.city_name, i.invoice_balance
FROM Customer_Table c, Invoice_Table i
WHERE (c.city_name = "Versailles" OR "Paris")
  AND c.customer_no = i.customer_no;
```

An important aspect of relational query processing is optimization of join access. A slow way to join two tables is to process sequentially the rows of one table, scanning the other to find the row(s) with the same join-key value. Faster techniques use table sorts, indexes, and other forms of directories. Join processing is essentially runtime computation of value-based relationships.

An important aspect of the relational operators is that they form a closed system. All operators act on tables and produce tables. Thus the programmer can combine and nest operators in powerful ways with predictable results. An example of nested SELECTs follows:

```
T6 = SELECT c.customer_no, c.city_name, i.invoice_balance
FROM Customer_Table c, Invoice_Table i
WHERE (c.city_name = "Versailles" OR "Paris")
   AND c.customer_no = i.customer_no;
   AND c.birth_date IN
      (SELECT f.birth_date
        FROM Famous_musicians_Table f
        WHERE f.birth_place = "France");
```

This request might be useful in selecting customers to include in a special promotion program celebrating both French musicians and customers with auspicious birthdates.

SQL provides flexible access to tables: it poses no limitations on what columns can be projected, what restrictions can be applied, or how tables can be combined. Even bizarre requests can be easily stated; for example:

```
SELECT c.customer_name
FROM Customer_Table c, Zoo_animal_Table z
WHERE c.no_of_children = z.no_of_legs
   AND c.eye_color = z.eye_color;
```

This request joins the `Customer_Table` and `Zoo_animal_Table` relations based on relationships phrased in terms of `no_of_children`, `no_of_legs`, and `eye_color`. The meaning of these relationships is not entirely clear.

The "safest" joins, that is, those that are likely to reflect some valid real-world meaning, are based on columns that are specified as corresponding primary and foreign keys. These joins reflect relationships that are inherent in the semantics of the data. To find relationships, look for use of the REFER-ENCES clause in SQL definitions of table structures.

A developer can use a type in an object model as the basis for defining other types, which become subtypes. A subtype inherits all the characteristics of its supertype. Subtyping is not supported by a relational DBMS. Several examples in Chapter 5 will show some difficulties programmers may encounter trying to store even a simple type–subtype hierarchy in a relational database.

Many applications need extensible typing. For example, a financial institution may have a product line of derived securities. The firm can gain competitive advantage by bringing new kinds of securities to market as quickly as possible. The firm can derive many of these new securities directly from existing securities. There may be a family of mortgage or bond products that are all quite similar yet that differ in certain characteristics. Type inheritance facilitates modeling the common and dissimilar nature of the securities.

There are similar situations in other industries, including

- manufacturing, where a company offers families of similar products

- insurance, where an agency issues similar (but slightly different) kinds of policies

- human resources, where a benefits package contains a choice of similar coverages

- health care, where conditions and treatments can be classified by similarities, with derived differences.

Because the relational table model does not include type inheritance, the developer must code all the logic for type hierarchy relationships into the application code. If each type maps to a table, the application developer has to understand somehow into which tables to insert when adding an object to the database. If a hierarchy is collapsed into a single table, the application developer has to understand which columns to fill and which to leave null for a particular record. Chapter 5 gives examples of these mappings and the corresponding program logic.

Extensible typing moves semantics from applications into the database framework. However, the more often that application developers code type semantics into applications instead of having the DBMS enforce the semantics, the greater the likelihood that the database will be corrupted by the applications. Putting semantic responsibility into the DBMS avoids inconsistent enforcement of semantic constraints by different applications.

Because an object DBMS supports both type inheritance and type extensibility, database administrators and programmers can define new types quite easily. A primary constraint on type definition is typically the programming language environment. For example, because C++ is an inherently static, compiled environment, object database type extensions in the C++ environment generally require affected class specification files to be recompiled. If that same object DBMS also supports Smalltalk, it probably supports dynamic type definition.

OBJECT DBMSs SUPPORT RELATIONSHIPS DIRECTLY

An object model includes relationships between objects. These relationships, which are associations between objects, are like the relationships between entities in entity–relationship (ER) data modeling; see [Bruc92] and [Chen76]. An object model may also include containment relationships and recursive structures. An object DBMS builds these relationships into the object database and can use them directly at runtime when returning objects to applications. By contrast, a relational DBMS must recreate relationships at runtime using joins, based upon instructions from an application. As a result, object DBMS products can generally perform better than relational DBMSs for applications that require traversal of relationships. An example in Chapter 5 uses geometry to show why complex relationships perform better with an object database than with a relational database.

The relationships in ER data models are purely abstract, while object databases carry relationship semantics into implementation. For example, consider the following relationship descriptions:

- There is a one-to-one equipment–use relationship between flight segments and aircraft. A particular flight segment on a given day uses one and only one aircraft.

- There is a one-to-one departure relationship between flight segments and airports, and another one-to-one arrival relationship between flight segments and airports. Each flight segment has exactly one departure airport and one arrival airport.

- There is a one-to-many publication relationship between publishers and books. Each publisher can publish many books, and each book can be published by only one publisher.

- There is a many-to-many authoring relationship between papers and people. Each paper can be authored by one or more people, and each person can author one or more papers.

These relationships can be built into the object database implementation such that joins between tables are not needed to reconstruct the relationships at runtime. The object DBMS can also enforce cardinality semantics (e.g., one-to-one, one-to-many, many-to-many) when objects are inserted into or removed from participation in a relationship.

Another example that includes relationships is time-series data, which is prevalent in a wide variety of applications. Financial portfolio analysis makes extensive use of histories of stock performance through various periods, with each selected date or time being a point in the time series. Clinical pharmaceutical studies to measure the effectiveness of new drugs also collect time-series data measuring various conditions and parameters. Patient information systems collect time-series data on vital signs and treatments. Shop floor control systems collect time-series data on inventory and production levels.

Relational databases are not well suited to manipulating this kind of data. In relational theory the ordering of rows in a table is explicitly immaterial. The argument is that a table contains the same information, regardless of the order in which its rows appear. This is a valid perspective, unless the ordering itself is supposed to convey information. Storing time-series data in a relational table implies storing the sequence information explicitly in the table, typically as a column whose values represent the sequence. To run through the rows in the time-series sequence requires the relational DBMS to sort the rows. Even though much effort has been expended in the development of highly efficient sort algorithms, sorting is still a relatively slow process, especially for large tables.

By contrast, an object database can store sequenced objects in an ordered collection, say in a list. The elements of the list are linked in the expected sequence, and the object DBMS can quickly follow the links at runtime. The relationships between the objects are stored in the database, and the object DBMS can use them at runtime. The object DBMS does not need to recreate logical paths. The part geometry and polyline example in Chapter 5 illustrates the differences in code required to traverse a set of line segments in a particular sequence in a relational database and in an object database.

CONTAINMENT IS ANOTHER FORM OF INTEROBJECT RELATIONSHIP

Another form of relationship that an object database can store directly but that is difficult for a relational database to represent is containment. Containment relationships are sometimes named "contains," "has," "comprises," or "is made of" in ER or object models. For example:

- An order is made of line items for particular products.

- A folder contains files.

- A state contains counties.

- A part is made of subparts.

- A document has an abstract, a table of contents, chapters, references, and an index.

- A chapter is made of a sequence of paragraphs and figures.

- A paragraph is made of a sequence of sentences.

- A sentence is a sequence of words.

- A word is a sequence of characters.

Containment has special semantics, in that there can be properties and operations that apply to the container as a whole. For example, a document container might have font and size attributes, which apply to all contained objects unless overridden. Containers also have special delete and copy semantics. Deleting or copying the container implies deleting or copying the contents of the container. Object DBMS products vary in the degree of support they give to containers.

Relational databases can store containers as blobs (binary large objects), but internal structures of the containers are lost. This loss means that encoding and detection of the internal structure of the container becomes an application responsibility. A text editor must encode a document's structural information explicitly in the document. Reading or modifying the document requires the application to decode the document's structure. By contrast, an object database could store the document as a container object, and the object DBMS could understand the structure of that container. A document is an object composed of other objects. An application can request access to a particular component object, say the list of references or a specified chapter, without having to decode markers in the bits stored as a document blob.

Product definitions are container objects in computer-aided design (CAD) and computer-aided software engineering (CASE) applications. If the product is software, then the product definition may consist of requirements models (data models, process models, timing models), design specifications, source code, executable code, test data, test result suites, performance data, and information about the development environment (version of the compiler, hardware platform, and so forth). Each of these objects may be a container of finer-grained objects. A CASE environment needs to be able to manage related objects as a container, as well as provide access to the component objects and the whole. If the product is a mechanical or electronic part, then the product definition may consist of different kinds of requirements models, design specifications, geometry data, test data, test result suites, performance data, and so forth, but the concept is the same as for software products. A mechanical CAD (MCAD) or electronic CAD (ECAD) environment needs to be able to manage related objects as a container, as well as provide access to the components at any level.

Historically, the vendors of MCAD and ECAD products found the relational DBMSs simply too slow to meet their performance requirements and instead used the file system solution to give persistence to their application "objects." The design of a product was subdivided into parts, and each part's geometry was developed in a separate model file. Sometimes designers used a model-file naming scheme and off-model reference notation to represent the hierarchical structure of parts within a product. The CAD requirements for fast traversal of product geometry relationships to satisfy stringent graphical-display performance expectations simply could not be met by the relational DBMSs. The unsatisfactory performance of the relational DBMSs was due partly to their having to recreate the relationships among container objects at runtime. The MCAD and ECAD markets have gradually evolved to the point where some products now support multi-engineer design environments, rather than single-user workstations. As the vendors looked for ways to move database capabilities into their products, they found that object DBMSs could meet both their performance and database functionality needs.

A RECURSIVE STRUCTURE IS A SPECIAL KIND OF CONTAINMENT

A special kind of container relationship that object databases support directly is recursive structures. Probably the most well known of these is the bill-of-materials structure, or the part–subpart structure. A typical data model for the bill of materials is shown in Fig. 3-2.

Recursive structures can be represented in a relational database, but they are complex for an application to process. A table structure for the part–subpart hierarchical structure might be as follows:

```
Part_Subpart_Hierarchy (this_part_id, contains_part_id)
```

Traversing the parts hierarchy with SQL requires that the application start with a particular `this_part_id` value, and select all the rows with that specified value for `this_part_id`. Then for each `contains_part_id` value in that set the application must find the rows where the `contains_part_id` value is equal to the `this_part_id` value. Then the rows for all their `contains_part_id` values must be located, and so forth. Each level of recur-

FIGURE 3-2.
BILL-OF-MATERIALS DATA MODEL.

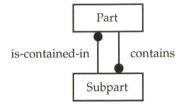

sion requires searching the table to find the rows where the `contains_part_id` value at one level equals the `this_part_id` value at the next level, being careful of course to stop correctly when `contains_part_id` values are null. Did you follow all that? This continues until all levels of containment have been searched, and it is far from trivial to code.

By contrast, an object DBMS can structure the part–subpart relationships directly in the object database. The application can traverse those relationships without instructing the object DBMS to recreate them at runtime. The performance implications can be significant [Catt92].

THE RELATIONAL MODEL IS BEING EXTENDED TO CAPTURE ADDITIONAL SEMANTICS

There has been considerable work to extend the relational model to capture additional semantics; for example, see [Codd79]. The SQL standards committee, ANSI X3H2 and ISO, are considering extensions to SQL92 [ANSI92] that would include object-oriented capabilities [Melt94]. In addition, some of the relational vendors are shipping extensions to the SQL model with their stored procedures and blobs features.

None of the attempts to extend SQL to date has been sufficient to transform a relational DBMS into an object DBMS. Extending SQL still keeps the SQL interface distinct from the programming language, even when extended SQL is embedded in an object programming language. This form of extension does not necessarily appeal to the object programmer, who seeks seamless integration between the source of persistence and the programming environment. Recall from Chapter 2 that object programmers generally want the database to be as invisible as possible. They want the database interface to be the object programming language, not SQL or a derivative of

SQL. However, extensions to SQL are likely to be welcomed by the MIS community, which is already familiar with SQL and wants the capability to use relational databases to support media-rich applications.

Successful extension of SQL to objects will require that the SQL data model and operators not be confined to dealing with sets. Extending the relational operators to include non-set operators will require significant changes to some relational DBMSs. They will need to support dynamic types and complex data as well as method invocation. SQL may become a complete programming language, or the relational DBMSs will have to work more closely with programming language environments to support active databases.

DATABASE PEOPLE ALSO EXPECT CLASSICAL DBMS FUNCTIONALITY

In addition to the fundamental expectation that an object DBMS supports objects, the basic set of requirements imposed on object DBMS products by the database management perspective is that *an object DBMS is a DBMS.* Being a DBMS means supporting the classical DBMS functions—storage management, schema management, concurrency control, transaction management, recoverability, query processing, and access control. These features protect databases as resources separate from any individual's use. Note that single-user PC DBMS products are a relatively degenerate case of DBMS as defined here. They do not support multiuser access, and they have no concurrency control or transaction management capabilities.

A database is by definition a persistent resource; Chapter 2 explained that persistence is typically the fundamental reason that object programmers want to use an object database. An object DBMS provides efficient storage management for both built-in and application-defined types. Storage management is important because it is a major factor determining database performance. Supporting persistence means providing efficient ways to represent and access both small and large volumes of objects on nonvolatile storage media. Over the years the database community has developed techniques for structuring databases, providing "fast paths" to database contents, clustering portions of databases that are likely to be accessed together, and managing databases that spread across many physical devices. Object DBMSs use these techniques and others in managing database storage.

A DBMS must understand the structure and semantics of a database (i.e., its schema) in order to provide access and enforce semantics. An object database schema manager works closely with the object programming language type definition facility. Schema management is important because it allows database structures to change as requirements change, without requiring large efforts to load and reload databases. A relational database schema is specified using SQL and managed entirely within the realm of the relational DBMS. In contrast, an object database schema is specified using an object programming language and is closely related to the application's type hierarchy. The object DBMS schema manager provides a fundamental link between the database and programming language environments.

Even though a fundamental principle of object technology is the close coupling of data structure and applicable operations into objects, most object DBMS products currently manage only states, in the form of data structures (see Fig. 3-3), leaving the behavioral aspects of objects to the object programming languages. An object DBMS that supports C++ typically requires that operations be coded in C++ and stored in .cxx files to be linked with the application.

Among exceptions are Servio's Gemstone and Hewlett Packard's

FIGURE 3-3.
STORING OBJECT DATA STRUCTURES VERSUS STORING OBJECTS.

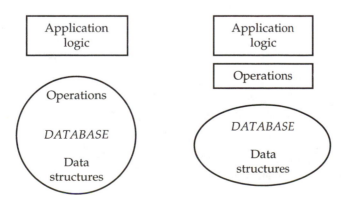

OpenODB. Both products store and execute operations in the database engine rather than the application space. Early versions of Gemstone did this by offering a Smalltalk-like language (Opal) to implement persistent classes. Database methods were coded in Opal, which the Gemstone engine could execute. Opal has evolved to become essentially Smalltalk. OpenODB provides its own object programming language (OSQL) to implement persistent classes. Just as a relational DBMS can execute commands written in SQL, OpenODB can execute operations written in OSQL.

The benefits of avoiding the artificial split between an object's data structures and operations by actually storing objects in an object database are

1. improved management and administration of code modules, rather than requiring code to be linked with applications, and

2. increased flexibility in specifying where operations execute in a network.

The reason that most object DBMS products do not store complete objects is to benefit from close coupling with the object programming language environment. In the future, more object DBMSs may evolve to include C++ or Smalltalk execution engines. They might then be referred to as active databases [Beer91], [Vorw94].

MULTIUSER CONCURRENCY CONTROL IS EXPECTED

A database is a shared resource, accessible by multiple users and/or applications. Object sharing features are important because they determine whether multiple users can safely access objects concurrently. Using the file system for persistent storage of objects does not provide protected sharability. File-based persistence is suitable for single-user applications, but not for shared collections of objects. Object sharing is provided by a combination of object DBMS techniques, which are usually referred to as concurrency control and transaction management features. Transaction management includes database recoverability capabilities.

Concurrency control is fundamental to an object DBMS's ability to support sharing. Without concurrency control, users can interfere with each other, jeopardizing database integrity. Whenever two or more users are simultaneously accessing a database and at least one of them is doing updates (i.e., adding, changing, or deleting objects), there can be interference, which can result in inconsistency. Interference occurs because concurrent users of a database may find their actions interleaved.

For example, consider two transactions. Transaction A intends to add 5 to the value of x and transaction B intends to multiply the value of x by 2. Assume that the initial value of x is 10. Transactions A and B start at nearly the same time and both read the value of x as 10. Transaction A updates its working copy of x and stores 15 in the database. Transaction B, meanwhile, updates its working copy of x and stores 20 in the database. x can have only one value at a time in the database: the latest value that was stored. The effect is the loss of transaction A's update, which could have been avoided if transaction B had been unable to read the value of x until after transaction A's update completed.

Providing concurrency control means guaranteeing that transactions are serializable: the result must be the same as some serial (i.e., non-interleaved) execution of the same transactions. Instead of 20, x should have the value 30 or the value 25, depending on whether transaction A or B were to complete first. Both values are correct in the perspective of the DBMS.

QUERY PROCESSING IS EXPECTED

Database people expect object DBMSs to support queries. Query processing supports efficient declarative access to objects, independent of procedural aspects of a programming language. There are a variety of techniques for querying object databases. All include the traditional relational notions of querying based on value, augmented by the ability to query based on relationships and values that result from method execution. Some query facilities are closely coupled with object programming languages, and in fact use the object programming language directly as the query language. Other facilities stand alone or leverage SQL syntax. All query processors must pay attention to query optimization, especially with databases containing large volumes of objects.

Another fundamental dimension of DBMS functionality is providing security and access controls. This is an area of some weakness for today's object DBMS products. For example, none meets the standards of government certification for security. Most rely in large part on the underlying operating system, typically Unix or Windows, for security mechanisms. Many use a password-protection scheme on opening databases but provide no additional controls at the object or member-of-object levels. This is an area where the relational DBMS products are generally more advanced than their object DBMS counterparts.

DATABASE TOOLS ARE EXPECTED

The database manager perspective also adds expectation of the availability of database administration and application development tools. Only rarely do relational DBMS customers buy only a DBMS engine; they usually also buy accompanying tools. Some tools help them configure and control the database environment. Others assist the application development process. Both kinds of tools are designed to work well with the relational DBMS. Database people increasingly expect availability of the same kind of "whole product" support with the object DBMS engines.

Database administration and application development tools typically support the following actions:

- Determining which objects are stored where, and relocating them as needed to balance resource loads and provide availability

- Declaring who can access which objects and for what purposes, and changing those access privileges as needed

- Measuring a wide range of performance and usage statistics and tuning system resources as required

- Viewing schemas and/or instances and graphically creating schemas

- Using forms-based application generators, report writers, and visual-programming tools.

Database people expect the tools for object databases to be comparable to those found in the relational market. In general, however, the object database tools still need time to mature.

Tools for developing object database applications necessarily work closely with object modeling tools, object programming environments, and GUI builders. Customers may integrate tools from multiple vendors to customize their own tools environments, or use an integrated set of application development tools from a single vendor. In contrast, developers typically expect database administration tools to come directly from the object DBMS vendor.

OBJECTS ARE THE NEXT STEP IN DATABASE MANAGEMENT EVOLUTION

Each generation of database management technology has leveraged from its predecessors and added capabilities of particular value. This chapter has emphasized the point that object databases represent an incremental step from relational technology: the added value is object model support; the retained value is classical DBMS functionality. In fact, object DBMSs leverage the contributions of the generations prior to relational DBMSs as well.

The first generation of database managers were the network and hierarchic DBMSs (see Fig. 3-4). They were developed in the mid-1960s in response to the basic need to have data storage that could be accessed in multiple ways and shared by multiple programs. The primary contribution of using these DBMSs instead of a file system for persistence is that they enabled data to become a shared resource rather than being captive to individual programs. The most famous of the network and hierarchic generation of database managers includes IBM's IMS and DL/I products, Cincom's TOTAL product, Hewlett-Packard's Image and TurboImage products, and

FIGURE 3-4.
DATABASE MANAGER GENERATIONS [Loom91c].

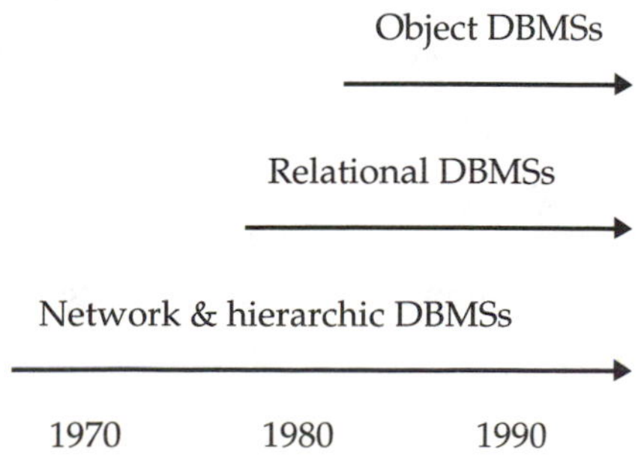

Object DBMSs

Relational DBMSs

Network & hierarchic DBMSs

1970   1980   1990

the CODASYL-compliant products from a variety of other vendors (IDMS from Cullinet, DBMS from Digital, IDS from Honeywell, and so forth). Most of these products are for mainframe computers; some are midrange products. Nearly all were introduced in the late 1960s or early 1970s.

The network and hierarchic DBMSs have their own data definition and data manipulation languages, and they support multiple types of records (e.g., Department, Employee, Project, and Skills) interrelated in fairly rigid structures. Occurrences of each type of record typically can be accessed either sequentially or using an access key. The DBMSs provide index structures, hash tables, and interrecord pointers. The databases can be quite efficient in response to the kinds of access that they were designed to support. Their structures are relatively difficult to change, and programming accesses for new applications can be a time-consuming proposition. Years of experience are usually required for a "database person" to be considered an IMS expert.

Network and hierarchic DBMSs provide all the classical DBMS functions except query processing. This capability and the simple table model were the main added values of the second-generation database managers—the relational DBMSs. The most famous of the relational DBMS products include Oracle, IBM's DB2 and SQL/DS, Sybase's SQLServer, Ingres, and Informix. Relational DBMSs became quite popular in commercial data processing in the second half of the 1980s. The relational products lost some of the previous generation's capability to represent interrecord relationships directly in databases.

The object DBMSs leverage the best of their predecessors, while attempting to avoid some of their difficulties. For example, the built-in relationship capability important to object databases directly leverages the interrecord navigational capability of the network and hierarchic DBMSs. The object DBMSs, however, introduce new techniques for implementing relationships that avoid the physically dependent pointer techniques of the first generation. Similarly, the query functionality of object DBMSs directly leverages the query capabilities of relational DBMSs. The object DBMSs, however, introduce new techniques to exploit the power of the object model and integrate the query language into the programming language environment.

The object DBMSs also extend the classical DBMS notion of transactions and extend sharing capabilities to include functionality for use of databases in collaborative work environments. For example, multiple processes may need to be involved in a single transaction. A transaction may be quite long, for instance, to accommodate logical units of work that encompass entire design sessions. There may need to be multiple coexisting versions of an object, each used in different aspects of a collaborative effort.

COEXISTENCE OF GENERATIONS IS ESSENTIAL

It is important to understand that generations of database managers never die; they persist forever. Hierarchic DBMSs are still in widespread use, eclipsed only by use of the file system! Many large data processing organizations are still contemplating the introduction of relational DBMS technology. Object DBMSs will coexist with other kinds of database managers for a long time to come. It is important to understand the characteristics of each generation and the kind of applications best suited to each.

Relational DBMSs tend to be used for database applications with the following characteristics:

- simple data that can be represented in tables using the built-in data types supported by the relational DBMSs

- flexible access which can be phrased simply using the value-based constructs of SQL

- simple transactions that the DBMS can process in short periods (i.e., milliseconds).

The largest class of these applications is called *on-line transaction processing* (OLTP). These applications include systems that support large quantities of automatic teller machines, airline reservation agents, financial floor traders, and many management information systems (MIS) applications.

By contrast, object DBMSs tend to be used for database applications with the following characteristics:

- complex data that is highly interrelated and/or includes multimedia data types

- high-performance needs with predictable access patterns and localized working sets

- distributed computing environments, which commonly involve collaborative work, long transactions, and versioning.

The majority of these applications today are in CAD, CASE, telecommunications, financial services, and geographic information systems (GIS). The industry is moving steadily toward substantial use of object databases in innovative MIS applications.

IN CLOSING . . .

The primary contribution of object databases from a database manager's perspective is object model support. It is precisely this liberation from the relational table model that enables object databases to be an integral part of object technology. Object model support simplifies application development. The synergy between the object programming language and an object DBMS typically results in fewer lines of code to store and access objects in an object database than in a relational database [Loom93b]. The benefits of fewer lines of code are expected to include

- better software quality, because fewer lines mean fewer opportunities to introduce defects

- easier software maintenance, because fewer lines make code easier to understand

- better programmer productivity, because fewer lines involve less work

- shorter development times, again because fewer lines entail less work.

Object model support enables developers to use object DBMS technology to tackle database applications for which records, relational tables, and limited data types are unsuitable. These applications typically require recursive structures, user-defined dynamic network or hierarchical structures, directed acyclic graphs, navigational access, or other structures with inherently ordered elements and logic to be applied sequentially at each element.

The combination of object model support and classical DBMS functionality helps object DBMSs meet database people's expectations for high-performance database support of complex, multiuser applications.

CHAPTER 4

Object Databases and Programming Clashes

Chapters 2 and 3 considered object databases from the dual perspectives of object programming and database management. A basic premise has been that object technology blurs the boundaries between these traditionally distinct software disciplines. Object databases have roots in both programming languages and database managers. This multidisciplinary heritage can deliver certain benefits, like the boost in productivity accruing from a consistent object model that could not otherwise be achieved with the multimodel, multilingual vaulting approach.

However, not all aspects of the programming language and database management technologies blend together easily in object DBMS products. There are potential conflicts and issues in areas of interface transparency, query scope, transaction management, object lifetimes, dynamics, control, and object model components. Not all the object DBMS vendors have used the same approaches in reconciling differences in the programming language and database management perspectives. Understanding these differences should help you better understand the various object DBMS products. The clashes are even more pronounced between the object programming languages and the relational and extended-relational DBMSs.

ARE THE PROGRAMMING AND DATABASE LANGUAGES THE SAME OR DIFFERENT?

The traditional database view is that persistent data is external to and independent of applications. Databases are "out there" and programmers should be explicitly aware of them. The database philosophy is that programmers should know when they are dealing with database objects and when they are dealing with program objects, and should expect to treat them differently. Programmers traditionally manipulate databases with a language provided by the DBMS, that is used only for database access.

Database people expect that the database language will be programming-language neutral. For relational databases this neutral language is SQL. For some applications, the SQL executes independently, typically in an interactive form. For other applications, the SQL statements execute in the context of a programming language. SQL is basically the same, regardless of whether it is embedded in C, FORTRAN, COBOL, C++, or Smalltalk.

How does this differ from the programming language philosophy? Chapter 2 explained that the object programmer expects an object database to be invisible. She expects to treat both transient and persistent object with a single syntax—the syntax of the object programming language. The notion of embedding a separate database language—SQL—in the midst of C++ or Smalltalk is not a natural one. The programmer expects to use the object programming language to define and access both transient and persistent objects. The programmer expects to treat all objects as if they resided in an unlimited virtual memory. Just as modern operating systems and language environments shield programmers from details of virtual memory, so also should the object DBMS shield programmers from details of an unlimited virtual memory containing both transient and persistent objects (see Fig. 4-1).

Why this difference in perspectives? One reason that database people traditionally have held the separate-language philosophy is so that applications written in any programming language can access a database, regardless of what other programming languages might also be used with that database. SQL serves as the programming-language–neutral interface to the database.

By contrast, the programming language point of view typically stems from a single-language perspective, sometimes even a single-user single-language perspective. Without a need to share objects across languages, there is little motivation for a programming-language–neutral database interface. Use C++ directly to access persistent C++ objects; use Smalltalk directly to access persistent Smalltalk objects.

Most of today's object DBMS vendors have adopted the programming language perspective on this interface issue. Rather than introducing a

FIGURE 4-1.
EXTENDING VIRTUAL MEMORY.

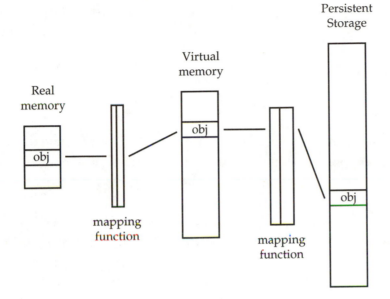

separate database language, their object DBMS products use the object pro-gramming language as the database schema definition and manipulation language. The object programmer is not required to learn and use an analog to SQL.

Some object DBMSs support multiple programming languages, with various degrees of sharability of the objects across the languages. In the simplest case, there is no sharing. An object created in C++ and stored in the object database can be manipulated only by C++ methods, not by Smalltalk methods, and vice versa. Two basic approaches to making objects sharable across the languages are as follows:

1. Store objects in the database in a programming-language–neutral format. Manifest objects from the neutral format to C++ or Smalltalk (or other) format on demand at runtime.

2. Store objects in the database using the format of the programming language that creates them. Transform objects as necessary to other language formats as needed at runtime.

These approaches to multilingual accessibility have performance trade-offs. The determination of which is the more appropriate approach should be influenced by the extent to which objects are actually required to be shared across languages and the number of different languages that the object DBMS is intended to support.

- If much cross-language sharing is required, then the first approach is more appropriate. If little cross-language sharing is required, then the second approach is more appropriate.

- If there are many languages to support, then the first approach is more appropriate. If there are just two languages to support, then the second approach is more appropriate.

Not unexpectedly, the vendors of relational and extended-relational DBMS products adopted the traditional database perspective instead of the programming language perspective on the "one language or two?" issue. They have a large vested interest in SQL and would rather add object-orientedness to SQL than help SQL fade into history.

WHAT IS THE QUERY LANGUAGE?

Another area of controversy between the database manager and programming language perspectives is query languages. A major contribution of relational database technology is its set-at-a-time query capability. Developers write SQL SELECT statements to specify predicates, i.e., WHERE clauses, which the DBMS uses to filter tables and find qualifying rows. The issue of coupling the SQL set-at-a-time operations with record-at-a-time programming languages was addressed in the late 1970s when SQL was embedded in COBOL and FORTRAN. The application declares cursors, which are like placeholders, and loops through a buffer of the records returned from a SELECT, applying programming language operations to each.

Predicate-based access is also an important way to access object databases. Many early users of object databases did not really care whether or not there was a query facility. Many were moving to use of object databases from files and had no experience with SQL. Increasingly, however, C++ and

Smalltalk programmers are finding value in predicate-based access. The database manager perspective has always considered the ability to query object databases important.

The object DBMS products that work with C++ may take three different language approaches to providing query capability:

1. standard C++, which calls query functions from C++

2. extended C++, which adds query syntax to standard C++

3. extended SQL, which adds object-orientedness to SQL and embeds the resultant language in standard C++.

There are several trade-offs among these approaches. The first can be accomplished with a wide variety of object programming compilers and debuggers. The first and second are quite natural to C++ programmers. The second is considerably cleaner than the first, but requires a preprocessor or extended compiler. The third requires a simple preprocessor and is natural to an SQL programmer, but may seem awkward to a C++ programmer. There are similar approaches for providing query capabilities in Smalltalk. Chapter 9 considers the three approaches in some detail.

The basic situation is that there are a variety of approaches to designing the query language interface to object databases. Most object DBMS vendors adopt a multilingual philosophy on this issue. They agree that the right answer to the question of how to provide query capability is with a variety of interfaces, each tailored for a particular kind of user. Thus you will find query facilities that blend seamlessly into a particular object programming language, stand-alone query facilities with an SQL flavor, and SQL-compatible query facilities that either stand alone or are embedded in the object programming languages.

HOW MUCH SQL IS ENOUGH?

Let's look at the third kind of query interface a little further. Once the decision has been made to embed an SQL-like interface in C++, there is another question to address: How much SQL is enough? SQL includes commands not only for queries, that is, for reading records, but also for deleting, updating, and creating persistent data, as well as for controlling other database operations such as transactions, access control, and database connections.

The relational database approach is to use SQL for all database operations. An application writes new database records using INSERT statements. DELETE statements remove database records. UPDATE statements change database record field values. Using the SQL approach could lead a C++ programmer to change a persistent instance of Student in a C++ program by saying

```
EXEC SQL UPDATE STUDENT s
  SET s.major_name("music")
  WHERE s.id_no===:next_student;
```

and to commit a transaction using

```
EXEC SQL COMMIT WORK RELEASE;
```

If an SQL-like interface were used for all operations against an object database, the C++ program would begin to look like it were using a relational database instead of an object database. The SQL-like interface would be used for manipulating persistent objects, and C++ would be used for manipulating transient objects. This result conflicts directly with the objective of seamless integration between the programming language and database environments. The object database would be no more integrated with the programming environment than a relational system is.

Recall that the programming language perspective expects that the developer will manipulate both persistent and transient objects with the object programming language. It expects that the developer will invoke all database operations (e.g., transactions, access control, and database connections) using the object programming language. Instead of introducing an SQL-like DELETE command, the programming language perspective is that all objects should be deleted by invoking the appropriate destructor. An application should change attribute values of persistent objects in exactly the same way that it changes values of any C++ object: using C++. Similarly, the programming language perspective dictates using the object programming language for other database operations. For example, a transaction is committed by:

```
transaction->commit();
```

Given these two extremes, how much SQL is enough? The object DBMS vendors do not yet agree on a single answer. The opinions seem to range from "no SQL is plenty of SQL" to "a future release of the product will support ANSI SQL," implying *all* of it, including UPDATE, INSERT, DELETE, COMMIT, and so forth. In between are various degrees of embedding the SQL SELECT statement. Some object DBMS products provide a select statement for queries, with the object programming language used directly for all other operations. The "no SQL" answer is most compatible with programming-language–driven products, while the "all of SQL" approach is most compatible with a database-driven philosophy.

When "all of SQL" is the answer, the vendor should consider carefully this auxiliary question: "why?" If the answer to that question is "to support existing SQL programs," then "all of SQL" may be the right answer. However, if the answer to "why?" is "to leverage SQL knowledge," then "part of SQL" may be the better answer. Leveraging SQL knowledge implies bringing object database capabilities to SQL-literate people for purposes of writing new applications. Thus only a judiciously chosen subset of SQL (perhaps only an SQL-like SELECT) needs to be supported.

Again the right answer to the original question of how much SQL is enough, is probably for the object DBMS to offer multiple interfaces: ranging from pure C++ for the C++ programmer to object extensions to SQL for the SQL aficionados. The object DBMS should ensure interoperability across the interfaces so that objects created with one interface can be manipulated using any of the other interfaces.

HOW INDEPENDENT ARE CONSIDERATIONS OF PERSISTENCE AND TYPE?

Other fundamental and related questions arise from a consideration of the appropriate degree of independence between persistence and type. At one extreme is the database manager's perspective that some functionality is pertinent only to persistent objects and not to transient ones. At the other extreme is the programming language perspective, which expects that all capabilities should be equally applicable to persistent and transient objects, regardless of their types.

Complete separation of persistence and type—the programming language perspective—is sometimes called *orthogonality of persistence and type* [Atki89]. Two axes on a graph are said to be orthogonal if they are perpendicular, that is, if they represent different dimensions. Similarly, persistence and type are considered to be orthogonal if they do not influence each other in any way: any type can have persistent or transient instances, and any behavior or characteristics that apply to a type are totally independent of whether its instances are persistent or transient.

Although many in the object database industry consider orthogonality of persistence and type to be desirable, none of today's object DBMS products completely implement this separation. Some interesting areas of interdependence occur in queries, schemas, transactions, existence semantics, and administration. Let's consider each of these.

SHOULD QUERIES APPLY TO BOTH PERSISTENT AND TRANSIENT OBJECTS?

Which objects should a query consider? Independent of the syntax used to specify predicate-based filtering, which objects should a query include in its scope? The traditional database point of view is that declarative queries (e.g., "select all the product designs Joe developed after September 15") should range over persistent objects, that is, over all the product designs that are stored in the *database.*

In contrast, the programming language point of view is that *persistence should be orthogonal to type* and that the programmer should treat both transient and persistent objects in exactly the same way. This view results in the conclusion that the range of a query should include both transient and persistent objects. Therefore, there should be no distinction that makes query capability applicable only to persistent objects.

If queries should apply to both transient and persistent objects, then does a given user's query need to filter the transient objects of the desired type that have been created in other user's applications but that have not yet been committed to persistent storage? Or does the user's query only include in its scope the transient objects of the desired type created by that run unit, along with appropriate persistent objects from the object database?

The object DBMS vendors have not arrived at a single answer to the query scope question. Some object DBMS products query only persistent objects; others query both transient and persistent objects. Including only locally transient objects and omitting the transients in other run units' address spaces is the typical approach taken by those object DBMSs that support queries to transient objects.

None of these approaches is inherently more correct than the others. Both the traditional database and programming language points of view are defensible. The semantics of the application really should be the determining factor for which approach is more convenient. In any case, to avoid unexpected results, it is important that programmers understand the approach used by their object DBMS.

Deciding that transient objects are included in query scopes complicates the design of the query processor. For example, the DBMS may need to construct and maintain indexes on transient as well as persistent objects. If queries include filtering of local transient objects, then the query processor must execute on the client application side and may even need to be distributed across the client and server processes. One object DBMS product proceeds to commit not-yet-committed instances prior to query execution, even if the enclosing transaction is not yet ready to commit. One reason to execute this intermediate commit is to enable processing of the query on a server process, rather than in the client application process.

SHOULD PERSISTENCE BE REFLECTED IN CLASS SPECIFICATIONS?

Persistence and type considerations are also reflected in the database management and programming language views of schemas. The traditional database point of view is that there should be explicit declaration of which types may have persistent instances. This viewpoint stems from a philosophy that persistent data and transient data are inherently different. The programmer should therefore be aware of when he is dealing with each. Database functionality, for example, queries, indexes, transaction commits, versions, and so forth, apply only to persistent objects. A DBMS should enforce semantic constraints, such as uniqueness and referential integrity, only for persistent objects. Since an object DBMS uses class specifications for its schema information, persistence capability should be explicitly declared in those class specifications.

By contrast, the programming language point of view is that all classes should be persistence-capable. There should be no distinction in either available functionality or mode of interface between transient and persistent objects, therefore there is no need to declare which classes are persistence-capable.

An object DBMS that takes the database approach of explicit declaration typically supplies a class (ODMG-93 [Catt94] calls it `Persistent_Object`) that provides persistent behavior. Any user-defined classes that are to have persistence capabilities are then derived from `Persistent_Object`. An advantage of the persistent base-class approach is that any overhead storage and processing necessary for persistent services need only be applied to persistence-capable classes. If there is a large proportion of types that will never have persistent instances, then avoiding this overhead may be important to system performance. A major disadvantage of the approach is that deriving from `Persistent_Object` means that an existing class hierarchy needs to be changed to work with the object DBMS. If the class hierarchy has been defined using C++, then the pertinent C++ source `.h` files need to be modified so that classes inherit appropriately from `Persistent_Object`. This derivation is complicated by use of third-party class libraries for which source code is not available.

An alternative approach implementing the programming language perspective is to make all classes persistence-capable. There is no explicit declaration in class libraries as to which classes may or may not have persistent instances, as all classes may. There is no special database functionality that applies to just some of the types. A major advantage of this approach is easier accommodation of existing C++ code and third-party class libraries. Because all classes may have persistent instances, these preexisting libraries can be used more directly with the object DBMS persistent storage mechanism.

SHOULD TRANSACTION SEMANTICS APPLY TO BOTH PERSISTENT AND TRANSIENT OBJECTS?

A related issue of the independence of persistence and type arises in transaction management. Programming language and database people alike generally agree that the commit of a transaction must guarantee that updates to persistent objects are durably written to persistent storage. Similarly, when a transaction aborts, any persistent-object updates that occurred during the transaction are guaranteed *not* to be written to the database. Database terminology characterizes persistent objects as *transaction-consistent*. The question is, what should happen to transient objects that were updated during an aborted transaction? Should these updates also be undone? Should object DBMSs support *transaction-consistent transient objects*?

The traditional database point of view ignores updates to transient objects. Because a DBMS does not manage transient objects, it does not log their updates and cannot undo them. Whatever changes were made in program memory variables remain, even if the transaction aborts. It is the application's responsibility to manage whatever clean-up may be required for program variables.

By contrast, the programming language view requiring consistency in treatment of transient and persistent objects leads to an expectation that the DBMS will also undo updates to transient objects. In fact, relatively strange things can happen if transient updates are not undone and the programmer is not careful. These anomalies commonly occur as bugs, for example, as variables that are not properly reset or counters that are not adjusted to account for aborted iterations.

Today's object DBMS products do not typically guarantee the transaction consistency of transient objects. One reason is that the overhead anticipated to deal with transient objects is expected to adversely affect object database performance. A compromise that allows transaction semantics to apply to transient objects when needed, without affecting general performance, may be for the object DBMS to provide an option for the programmer to flag selected transient objects for transaction-consistent treatment. Another option is to abandon the "persistence is orthogonal to type" objective here and just expect persistent and transient objects to behave somewhat differently with respect to transactions. It is important that programmers understand how transaction management and persistence management interact in the particular object DBMS they use.

SHOULD PERSISTENT OBJECTS BE GARBAGE-COLLECTED?

There also are differences in outlook about the existence semantics of objects. How long does an object exist and when is it actually deleted? This issue shows up when programmers use an object database with Smalltalk. In Smalltalk, an object exists if it is reachable, that is, if some other object references it. A Smalltalk object is garbage-collected, that is, removed from the Smalltalk Image, when it is no longer reachable.

The traditional database point of view, however, is that an object exists until it is explicitly deleted. Some future application may need to access a currently unreferenced object. Someone may need to pose a value-based query tomorrow that touches that particular object. It is not up to the DBMS to decide whether an object is garbage or not. DBMSs traditionally do not collect and destroy unreferenced objects.

Therefore, Smalltalk and traditional DBMSs have different existence semantics—different understandings of what is necessary for an object to exist. In Smalltalk, an object exists if it is reachable. To a DBMS, an object exists because it exists. Dealing with differences in existence semantics between Smalltalk and relational DBMSs can introduce rather significant logical challenges when a relational database is used to store Smalltalk objects [Loom94a].

One particular issue for the object DBMS vendor who wants to support Smalltalk is determining what the object DBMS for Smalltalk should include in an extent, which is the set of all instances of a class. Extents are commonly used as the scopes for queries. If the only reference to an object is because it is part of a class extent, does the object exist? One approach is for the object DBMS to treat the extent as a special kind of collection, the semantics of which include making an object eligible for garbage collection if its only reference is from the extent collector.

A related issue arises with the notion of keys, which are uniqueness constraints. A key is an (possibly compound) attribute, the value of which is unique across an extent. This is a database constraint notion that has been an integral part of the relational model. It is useful for entities with real-world unique identifiers, such as social security numbers, employee numbers, drawing numbers, expense-report numbers, and so forth. If a class has a defined key, the object DBMS should check that a new instance of that class does not violate the uniqueness constraint. Should it check both transient and persistent instances of the class? Should it check both transients local to this process and other transient instances of the class? Should it check again against only persistent instances at the end of the transaction? What if there is conflict with an about-to-be-garbage-collected instance's key value?

While most object DBMSs adopt the programming language perspective on tight integration of the database interface with the programming language environment, they adopt the traditional database management perspective and apply some operations (notably query, transaction consistency, indexes, and key constraints) to persistent objects only. Programmers who are using object databases with Smalltalk should pay special attention to the object DBMS's particular approach to managing extents and the interaction between transient and persistent objects.

SHOULD PERSISTENT OBJECTS BE SUBJECT TO ADDITIONAL CONTROLS?

Another interesting area of difference is control of persistent objects. The implications are primarily for schema management and access control. The programming language perspective is that applications should control class libraries. In fact, class libraries are sometimes controlled by individual programmers. In contrast, the database management perspective is that databases should be administered. They should not be controlled by applications, because databases are shared resources capable of supporting multiple applications.

Traditionally organizations with shared database applications have established a database administration (DBA) role. DBAs are responsible for database structures—for database schemas. With adoption of object technology by MIS organizations, the DBA role may evolve to a class library administration role. With object databases, schema definition is embodied in class libraries. Not only will the DBA ensure protection of the data aspects of persistent objects, but it will also ensure protection of their behavioral aspects. There must be a balance between having individual programmers ultimately responsible for the code they write, and establishing corporate control over corporate resources, which will increasingly include class libraries.

Access protection is another pertinent aspect of control. From a C++ point of view, members are either public, private, or protected. This characterization of members is really a software engineering practice and is not *security* in the database sense. Because of the single-user perspective dominant in the programming language community, C++ does not consider who the user is or what the application is, only the relationships of the classes. When there is only one user of a class, these levels of protection may be adequate.

In contrast, the database management perspective generally bases access protection not only on *what* is being requested, but also on *who* is making the request. For example, DBAs are authorized to make schema changes. Other users have read-only access to some parts of a database, while they can change other parts. Some relational DBMSs support access authorization at the field level; others protect at the row, table, or database level. Many support notions of roles and of users granting each other access rights.

The object DBMSs that support C++ generally use the C++ class specifications as the database-schema definitions. It is probably logical that the database should respect the same public, private, and protected notions as the language, but perhaps those levels of protection should be augmented with concepts of read and write authorization. Also, methods might be protected by requiring execute authorization. All object DBMS products currently require that attributes referenced in C++ queries be public.

Tight security controls were not implemented in the early object DBMS product releases, primarily because of the importance of getting product to market in a timely manner to start generating revenue, even if the ultimate functionality was not available in Release 1. Many of the early uses of object databases are in pilot and prototype projects, which do not typically have the same stringent levels of security protection requirements as some production systems. Security of object databases continues to be an area of active investigation. Some relational DBMSs provide much more extensive access protection.

WHAT SEMANTICS SHOULD BE INCLUDED IN AN OBJECT MODEL?

Although there have been many proclamations of the virtues of a common object model shared by the programming language and the object database, the programming language and database management points of view in fact have somewhat different expectations regarding what should be included in an object model.

The database management trend is to put increasing specification and enforcement of semantics into databases, taking that logic out of applications. Database people expect to be able to specify types, subtypes, relationships, attributes, integrity constraints, default values, null allowed/not, primary keys, and so forth. A DBA retains primary responsibility for the database semantics. The basic notion is that by increasing the semantic content of databases, the DBMS can consistently enforce semantic constraints across all applications that share the objects, and make the logic reusable by multiple applications.

By contrast, the object model of C++ or Smalltalk is relatively basic. For example, in C++ the * syntax is used to mean pointer implementation, without regard for the semantics between the objects involved. The programmer retains primary responsibility for semantics. Consider the following C++ class specification, which apparently includes a relationship between professors and departments:

```
class Professor
{ ...
  Department *dept;
... }
```

The database management point of view would insist on knowing more about the semantics of the department–professor relationship than can be deduced from the fact that a `Professor` instance contains a pointer to a `Department` instance. Many questions arise, including:

- Can a `Professor` instance exist without an associated `Department` instance, that is, can the pointer be null?

- If an application deletes a `Professor` instance, does the DBMS also delete the `Department` instance to which it points?

- If an application deletes a `Department` instance, does the DBMS also delete any `Professor` instances that point to the now-deleted `Department` instance? Does the DBMS somehow adjust pointers in the `Professor` instances?

- What is the maximum number of `Professor` instances that can point to a particular `Department` instance?

- What happens if a `Professor` instance can be related to more than one `Department` instance?

If the answers to these questions are not explicitly declared in the database schema, developers must code appropriate logic into applications to maintain integrity of the data. The database management point of view is that semantic integrity should as much as possible be the responsibility of the DBMS, not the programmer.

Object DBMS vendors tend to refer to relationships in terms of inter-object references. Some object DBMS products use C++ pointers, as in the preceding code, to denote these references. Others use parameterized types (templated classes) to represent references:

```
class Professor
{ ...
  Ref <Department > dept;
... }
```

ODMG-93 includes syntax for specifying the traversal paths and their inverses needed to associate the instances participating in a relationship, for specifying both bidirectional and unidirectional relationships, for specifying the cardinality of relationships (i.e., the number of instances that participate on either end of a relationship), and other semantics. For example:

```
class Professor
{
  Ref <Department> home_dept inverse Department::teaching_staff;
  Set <Ref <Student> > advisees inverse Student::advisor;
}
class Department
{
  Set <Ref <Professor> > teaching_staff inverse
       Professor::home_dept;
}
class Student
{
  Ref <Professor> advisor inverse Professor::advisees;
}
```

References between transient and persistent instances can be problematic. For example, the object DBMS implementor must decide what should happen to references to transient objects when a persistent object is written to the database. Should the transient pointer be nullified and raise an exception the next time it is used because the transient object may no longer exist? This is the ODMG-93 approach. Should the transient pointer be kept as is, even though it may refer to garbage the next time it is used? Should references to transient objects from persistent objects be disallowed? Some object DBMSs address these questions by making persistent all objects reachable by references from a persistent object. This approach typically is viable only if any class can have persistent instances; it does not work for systems that require derivation from a special class `Persistent_Object` to get persistence capability.

Even the fundamental notion that every object has a unique identifier is somewhat different from the programming language and database management points of view. To C++, an object identifier is an address in process memory space. This space is too small for most database purposes. To an object DBMS, an object identifier cannot be just a memory address. Scalability requires that object identifiers be valid across storage volumes. Distributed object databases require that object identifiers be valid across machine boundaries. From the database management perspective, an object identifier must be a unique identifier that persists with an object for its entire lifetime, regardless of where it may be stored or moved or how it is being used. The object DBMS can then use object identifiers as the basis of references used to implement relationships. However, from the programming language perspective, there should be no need to introduce reference syntax to supplement pointers. Pointers should be used instead of object identifiers or object identifiers should simply behave like pointers, even if the object DBMS eventually converts the addresses to the equivalent of object identifiers with a larger scope.

IN CLOSING . . .

The multifaceted technology legacy behind object databases sometimes poses tough questions that must be addressed by the object DBMS vendors. The challenge is to take advantage of the best each technology perspective has to offer, while minimizing the conflicts and inconsistencies. Understanding how the programming language and database management points of view differ should help you to better evaluate the tradeoffs made in the object DBMS products.

The programming language perspective tends to drive an object DBMS implementor to attempt to keep all functionality (including queries and transactions) applicable to all objects and to use class hierarchy directly as the database schema, without modification to incorporate derivation from an introduced class like `Persistent_Object`. The database management perspective tends to drive an object DBMS implementor to leverage SQL-like syntax into its query facility, to distinguish functionality (notably queries, transactions, and versioning) that is applicable only to persistent objects, and to provide tools for database administration and query facilities that can be invoked separately from object programs. Both perspectives have adopted the objective of tight integration of their interfaces with the object programming languages.

CHAPTER 5

Using a Relational DBMS with an Object Programming Language

At times it may be necessary to interface a relational DBMS with an object programming language. For example, an object application may need to access data that has already been stored in a relational database. Or an organization might be benchmarking an application on both object and relational DBMS products.

The integration of object databases and programming languages is in sharp contrast to the way that relational DBMSs work with their environments. This chapter focuses on the issues encountered in using a relational DBMS to store and manage objects. The challenges arise in the logic that developers must add to applications to make relational tables appear to contain objects.

USING A RELATIONAL DBMS WITH C++ REQUIRES MAPPING TABLES AND CLASSES

Because relational DBMSs have their own data model, there are certain constraints that the developer must face in using a relational database with an object programming language. These constraints stem primarily from the facts that:

1. Relational DBMSs support tables with a fixed set of types.

2. Intertable relationships are represented by common values.

3. Relational DBMSs support only set operations.

Many kinds of data can be stored in a relational database. If an application needs to store other, non–built-in (i.e., user-defined) types of data, that data might be stored in a blob or written to a file, with a reference to the file stored in an appropriate table in the database. The data written to the file is then not subject to the relational DBMS's capabilities for concurrency control, transaction management, recoverability, access control, and so forth. As Chapter 2 discussed, the application has responsibility for the logic to encode object structural information in blobs, or files, so that the structure can be retained.

Because relational DBMSs do not manage object models, the programmer has to write a large amount of otherwise unnecessary code to deal with semantic structures like inheritance and relationships. Consider the simple object model in Fig. 5-1. There are two types of employees: hourly and salaried. Each has its own specific attributes, and some attributes are common to all employees. To simplify things, ignore operations for now.

Using a relational DBMS for object persistence requires that the application map object models and relational models against each other. The object programming language understands only its object model. The relational DBMS understands only its table model. The two basic mapping tasks are

1. designing the tables to represent the data, and

FIGURE 5-1.
EXAMPLE TYPE HIERARCHY.

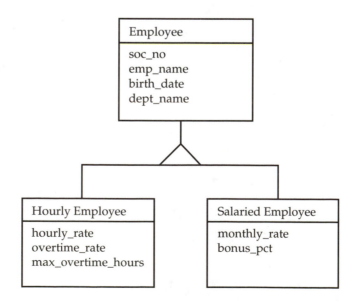

2. writing the code to transform the employee objects to table rows and vice versa.

There are several alternative approaches. The logic and code to transform objects to tables and vice versa are determined by which alternative is used for flattening and partitioning the objects into tables.

MAPPING CLASSES TO TABLES LOSES SEMANTIC INFORMATION

One approach is to map objects to tables with one table per class. The object model of Fig. 1-2 can be represented by three tables:

```
Employee_Table (soc no, emp_name, birth_date, dept_name)
Hourly_employee_Table (soc no, hourly_rate, overtime_rate,
  max_overtime_hours)
Salaried_employee_Table (soc no, monthly_rate, bonus_pct)
```

The fields participating in the primary key are underscored in each table definition. A prerequisite for this mapping is that the data types in the classes must be supported by the built-in relational data types.

The first problem with this representation is that semantic information has been lost in the mapping. The hierarchical inheritance structure has disappeared. From the three tables it is not clear which, if any, table represents the supertype and which the subtypes. It is not reasonable to expect the DBMS to deduce semantic meaning from the names of the tables. There is a possibility that the tables actually were named `Emp_A`, `Emp_B`, and `Emp_C`, or `foo`, `bar`, and `foobar`. It is not clear which tables should implicitly inherit attributes from other tables.

USING A RELATIONAL DATABASE CAN REQUIRE MANY LINES OF TRANSFORMATION CODE

The example object model indicates that employee is the supertype, and that the hourly employee and salaried employee subtypes inherit the attributes of employee. Because a relational DBMS does not support inheritance, this logic has to be programmed into application code. Let's see what the effort entails.

Let's write code to make a C++ employee object persistent in the relational tables. This mapping requires figuring out the type of the employee and inserting rows in the two appropriate tables.

```
/* the employee attribute values are already in the C++ object*/
EXEC SQL INSERT INTO Employee_Table
  (soc_no, emp_name, birth_date, dept_name)
  VALUES (:emp->soc_no, :emp->name, :emp->birth_date,
    :emp->dept_name);
if (emp->type == 1)
  EXEC SQL INSERT INTO Hourly_employee_Table
    (soc_no, hourly_rate, overtime_rate, max_overtime_hours)
    VALUES (:emp->soc_no, :emp->hourly_rate, :emp->overtime_rate,
      :emp->max_overtime_hours);
else if (emp->type == 2)
  EXEC SQL INSERT INTO Salaried_employee_Table
    (soc_no, monthly_rate, bonus_pct)
    VALUES (:emp->soc_no, :emp->monthly_rate, :emp->bonus_pct);
EXEC SQL COMMIT WORK RELEASE;
```

If you don't care to read the code, just notice that there are many more lines of it required than those needed to store that same C++ employee instance in an object database.

```
Transaction addEmp;
Ref <Employee> emp = new (database) Employee;
/* get values into emp attributes using C++ */
addEmp.commit();
```

With relational database storage, the programmer must code logic into the application correctly to ensure that fields are appropriately filled or left empty, that mutually exclusive tables (like `Hourly_employee_Table` and `Salaried_employee_Table`) stay that way, that each row representing a subtype instance has a corresponding row in the supertype table, and so forth. Because the object DBMS shares the C++ inheritance model, the object DBMS rather than the application deals appropriately with the subtyping hierarchy and stores the object semantics directly in the database.

MAPPING EACH LEAF CLASS TO A TABLE ALSO CAUSES SEMANTIC LOSS

Another approach is to map objects to tables with one table per leaf class. The supertype's attributes are then explicitly moved into the subtypes. Two tables suffice:

```
Hourly_employee_Table (soc no, emp_name, birth_date, dept_name,
  hourly_rate, overtime_rate, max_overtime_hours)
```

```
Salaried_employee_Table (soc no, emp_name, birth_date, dept_name,
    monthly_rate, bonus_pct)
```

This mapping also obscures the hierarchical inheritance structure, as it is not clear that the hourly employee and salaried employee types are subtypes of a single generic type. The programmer must code logic into the application to handle consistently the supertype parts of the two tables.

COLLAPSING THE HIERARCHY INTO A SINGLE TABLE CAN ALSO BE UNSATISFACTORY

Yet another approach is to collapse the inheritance structure into a single table:

```
Employee_Table (soc no, emp_name, emp_type, birth_date, dept_name,
    hourly_rate, overtime_rate, max_overtime_hours, monthly_rate,
    bonus_pct)
```

The programmer again bears responsibility for correctly assigning values to the appropriate attributes. Depending on the type of the employee object to be made persistent, some attributes should be null and others should be assigned nonnull values. For example, a salaried employee should have a null hourly rate and a nonnull monthly rate.

READING FROM TABLES CAN ALSO BE COMPLEX

The other part of the problem is writing the logic to bring relational data back into the object programming environment. Let's continue with the example, using the collapsed hierarchy mapping, with all subtypes represented in a single table. The code to load the data for the employees in the MIS department from the relational database includes the following fragment:

```
Department *d = new Department;
d->name = "MIS";
Employee *temp_emp = new Employee;
EXEC SQL DECLARE c1 CURSOR
    SELECT * FROM Employee_Table
    WHERE dept_name = "MIS";
EXEC SQL WHENEVER NOT FOUND GOTO end_of_table;
for(;;)    /* fetch rows until not_found is raised */
{
    EXEC SQL FETCH c1
        INTO :temp_emp;
```

```
if temp_emp->emp_type == 1
{   Hourly_employee *h = new Hourly_employee;
    h->soc_no = temp_emp->soc_no;
    h->emp_name = temp_emp->emp_name;
    h->birth_date = temp_emp->birth_date;
    h->dept_name = d;
    h->hourly_rate = temp_emp->hourly_rate;
    h->overtime_rate = temp_emp->overtime_rate;
    h->max_overtime_hours = temp_emp->max_overtime_hours;
}
else if temp_emp->emp_type == 2
{   Salaried_employee *s = new Salaried_employee;
    s->soc_no = temp_emp->soc_no;
    s->emp_name = temp_emp->emp_name;
    s->birth_date = temp_emp->birth_date;
    s->dept_name = d;
    s->monthly_rate = temp_emp->monthly_rate;
    s->bonus_pct = temp_emp->bonus_pct;
}
/* code to do something with the object */
}
```

Quite a few lines of code are required to handle correctly the typing information that is embedded in the relational table attribute values. Each `Employee_Table` row is read into a temporary instance of the `Employee` class, whose structure matches the row's. The type of the particular employee is used to determine how to instantiate the class hierarchy. Each employee object contains a pointer to the MIS department object, as well as a value for each of the appropriate attributes.

If the employee information were instead made persistent in an object database, the logic would reduce to:

```
Set <Ref <Employee>> MIS_Dept_Employees;
oql(MIS_Dept_Employees, "select ee from ee in Employees\
                        where ee.dept.name = \"MIS\" ");
/* code to do something with the objects, iterating over the set */
```

Each of the employee objects from the object database is automatically typed correctly for the C++ environment, because C++ and the object DBMS share the same type system. `Employee` and its subtypes are known to both C++ and the object DBMS. Each object read from the object database retains its type information as a C++ object.

MAPPING RELATIONSHIPS REQUIRES ADDITIONAL CODE WITH A RELATIONAL DATABASE

Here is another example that shows the effect on the programmer of using a relational DBMS for persistent storage of objects. Because the relational system does not understand relationships, extra logic has to be added to the C++ program, explicitly superimposing relationships on the basic table structure of a relational database.

This example uses the object model shown in Fig. 5-2. A polyline is a commonly used geometric construct composed of line segments, each of which contains line segments that connect points in three-dimensional space.

Let's first define polylines and part geometries in C++, and then compare the logic required to deal with these structures in an object database and a relational database. Skeletal C++ class definitions resemble the code on the following page.

FIGURE 5-2.
EXAMPLE OBJECT MODEL FOR POLYLINE EXAMPLE.

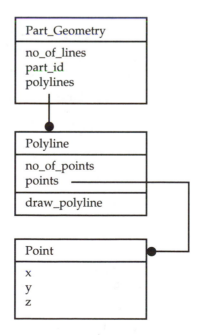

```
class Point
{
   public:
      double x, y, z;
}

class Polyline
{
   public:
      int no_of_points;
      List<Point> points;
      void draw_polyline();
      {   for (int i=0;i<no_of_points-1;i++)
              draw_line (points[i], points[i+1]);
      }
}

class Part_Geometry
{
   public:
      int no_of_lines;
      List<Polyline> polylines;
      string part_id;
}
```

Each `Polyline` object contains a list of sequenced points. A part geometry may include several `Polyline` objects.

To read a persistent part geometry from an object database and draw its lines, the application selects the part geometry of interest and then iterates through the geometry, invoking the `draw_polyline` function. `draw_polyline` draws the lines of the individual line segments; the next point in the list is the next point on the line. The C++ code for this follows:

```
Ref <Part_Geometry> g;
Set <Ref <Part_Geometry> > part_Geometries;
oql(g, "select g from g in part_Geometries\ where part_id =
    \"MyPart\" ");
for(int i=0, i<g->no_of_lines, i++)
{
    ref <Polyline> next_line = g->polylines[i];
    next_line->draw_polyline();
}
```

THE RELATIONAL MAPPING ADDS SEQUENCING ATTRIBUTES

The application differs considerably if it stores part geometries in a relational database instead of an object database. Let's consider mapping the object model to a relational database as four tables:

```
Part_geometry_Table (part id, no_of_lines)
Polyline_Table (polyline id, no_of_points, part_id)
Point_Table (point id, x, y, z)
Point_use_Table (polyline id, point id, sequence no, part id)
```

Polylines and points have been assigned the identifiers `polyline_id` and `point_id`, respectively, to fulfill the relational requirement for unique row identifiers comprised of field values and to simplify the code somewhat. The `sequence_no` field is needed because the relational DBMS cannot guarantee the ordering of rows in a table. The actual ordering of point rows in `Point_use_Table` may not correspond to the positions of the points on the polyline. The ordering of rows in a relational table is immaterial and sometimes unpredictable.

If there really should be a logical sequencing of the rows, say by time of insertion in the table or by the value of a particular column, or some other sequence, then that sequence must be captured in attribute values stored in the table rows. The relational DBMS will then use those values to recompute the logical ordering when an application needs to access the rows sequentially. SQL provides the ORDER BY clause for sorting the table rows resulting from a SELECT. Just as an intratable row relationship is represented by values in a sequence column of the table, intertable relationships are also represented by values in a relational database.

It is the application's responsibility to manage the introduced identifiers (`polyline_id` and `point_id`) and the sequencing field (`sequence_no`). This knowledge of the geometry thus is coded into the application rather than retained in the database.

READING THE GEOMETRY FROM A RELATIONAL DATABASE REQUIRES SELECTION, JOINING, AND SORTING

Using the preceding table definitions, let's now read a part geometry from the relational database. The application must supply the logic to obtain the points in sequence. We introduce a temporary `points` array to store the points of the line sequence for the C++ drawing process:

```
typedef struct (double x, y, z) Point;
Point points[1000];
int no_of_lines, max;
EXEC SQL SELECT pg.no_of_lines
    INTO :no_of_lines
```

```
        FROM Part_geometry_Table pg
        WHERE pg.part_id = "MyPart";
    for (int i=0, i<no_of_lines, i++)
    {
        EXEC SQL SELECT pl.no_of_points
            INTO :max
            FROM Polyline_Table pl
            WHERE pl.polyline_id = :i
                AND pl.part_id = "MyPart";
        int next_pt = 0;
        EXEC SQL SELECT p.x, p.y, p.z
            INTO :points[next_pt++]
            FROM Point_Table p, Point_use_Table pu
            WHERE p.point_id = pu.point_id
                AND pu.polyline_id = :i
                AND pu.part_id = "MyPart"
            ORDER BY pu.sequence_no;
        for (int j=0; j<max-1, j++)
        {
            draw_line(points[j], points[j+1]);
        }
    }
```

OBJECT DATABASES STORE RELATIONSHIPS DIRECTLY

Two very different kinds of processing are taking place in the relational and object databases, with significant productivity and performance implications. The example given in this chapter shows that considerably fewer lines of code are required using the object database for persistent storage of C++ objects. Fewer lines of code generally means more understandable, higher quality code, and more productive programmers. The mapping between C++ objects and database objects is trivial; the mapping between C++ objects and relational table rows can be complex.

As reflected in the relative numbers of lines of code, the relational processing is also more complex. After accessing the Part_geometry_Table, the C++ program searches through the table of polylines to find the particular one of interest and extracts its no_of_points value into the C++ variable max. Then Point_use_Table is joined with Point_Table on matching point_id values to select the points sorted by their ordinal position on the polyline. The x, y, and z values are copied into the temporary points array. The program then iterates through the points array, applying the draw_line method to each segment.

Joining and sorting typically compete for being the slowest operations in relational systems. Both are needed here. Joining two tables requires the

DBMS to find all pairs of rows from the two tables that have the specified match in attribute values. If one table has *n* rows and the other has *m* rows, the join may involve as many as *m*n* comparisons. In contrast, the object DBMS stores the references between polylines and points in the object database, preserving that information for use by multiple procedures and users and not having to recompute it using runtime joins and sorts for each one.

Another example of the need for a join to traverse a relationship arises using relational tables to store customer and account objects. Assume that the customer–account relationship is implemented by matching `customer_no` values in the `Customer_Table` and `Account_Table`. Using the relationship implies joining the two tables on those matching values. For example, to extract the address of the customer of a particular account requires the following:

```
SELECT c.customer_address
FROM Customer_Table c, Account_Table a
WHERE a.account_no = "A1234"
    AND a.customer_no = c.customer_no;
```

GATEWAYS FACILITATE ACCESS TO RELATIONAL DATABASES

Because the mappings between application objects and relational tables can be complex, it is generally good practice to isolate the mapping logic into a set of classes that give the relational database an object veneer. These classes can handle the tasks of interfacing with the relational DBMS and can contain classes for table, record, and cursor-related actions. These classes are sometimes called *gateways*. Encapsulating the mappings and relational DBMS interface work in low-level gateways can ease the development of object applications that need to access relational databases.

In effect, use of SQL and the relational storage mechanism is hidden in the implementation of a few classes. Each class might have a method for creating a corresponding table. There generally are classes like `SQL_Database`, `SQL_Table`, `SQL_Row`, and sometimes `SQL_Query`. There might be a **save** method and a **query** method for each class mapped into the relational database. These classes should be written by developers who are intimately familiar both with the application objects and the relational databases. Other developers can then be shielded from the mappings and SQL courtesy of the encapsulation of the logic in the gateway. For example, each class might have its own `insertIn` operation, implementing the SQL to insert rows in the appropriate relational tables.

There are a variety of gateway products available today that assist in construction of customized gateways. These products are available for both the Smalltalk and C++ environments. In general they provide facilities for the programmer to:

- connect to and disconnect from a relational DBMS

- create and destroy tables in a relational database

- build queries to insert, update, retrieve, and destroy data
  in a relational database [LaLo93].

Their objective is to simplify the object programmer's task of dealing with a relational database by minimizing the requirement to write SQL statements.

IN CLOSING . . .

Using a relational database for object persistence is not nearly as straightforward for the object programmer as is using an object database. However, there are situations where use of a relational database is required. For example, some data needed by the object program may already be stored in a relational database, and it may be unreasonable to replicate that data in an object database.

Using a relational database for object persistence must be done carefully, as the mapping between application objects and relational tables may be complex. The mapping can be accomplished most successfully by developers who are knowledgeable about the application objects, the semantics of the relational database, and the syntax of SQL. The developers can encapsulate transformation logic in low-level classes, to be reused by other programmers.

CHAPTER 6

An Object Model

One of the distinguishing characteristics of an object database is support for an object model. We have seen that this object model is important because it determines the kinds of information that can be stored in an object database and the semantics that the object DBMS can understand and enforce. This chapter explores in more detail the object model supported by object DBMSs.

THE OBJECT MODEL DESCRIBED HERE IS SUPPORTED BY A VARIETY OF OBJECT DBMS PRODUCTS

There have been numerous efforts to develop models that describe the semantics of objects. One ANSI committee (X3H7—Object Information Management) has devoted considerable effort to the development of an Object Model Features Matrix to compare and contrast various approaches [ANSI94]. As of 1994, X3H7 had profiled over a dozen object models, representing a multitude of object technology products and research efforts.

The object model described in this chapter was developed by the Object Database Management Group (ODMG) consortium of object DBMS vendors, in an attempt to develop a standard that would help ensure the portability of applications across their products and the eventual interoperability of their products. This object model is described in detail in Chapter 2 of the ODMG-93 specification [Atwo94], [Atwo93], [Catt94], [Loom93d], [Loom93e]. The work of the ODMG continues to evolve, so there may be some discrepancies between what is presented here and what is eventually published in later releases of that specification.

The ODMG object model was selected as the basis for this chapter for another reason: it is supported by commercially available object DBMS products. The member companies of the ODMG agreed to support the object model published in [Catt94]. The actual level of object model support provided by any particular object DBMS product is expected to evolve as new releases appear. ODMG-93 also includes chapters that define programming-language–independent facilities for defining types, an object query language, and C++ and Smalltalk interfaces for defining types and manipulating and querying objects.

THE ODMG OBJECT MODEL SEPARATES INTERFACE AND IMPLEMENTATION

Chapter 1 introduced the notion of objects as software building blocks. The interior of an object is private to the object, while its exterior is public and available for other objects to see or use. The exterior is called the object's *interface*. The interior is called its *implementation*. The interface of an object is an abstract specification; it does not dictate how the object is to be represented or otherwise implemented. A developer can define an object's interface, independent of the particular technology (e.g., programming language or database) eventually used to implement the object.

Each object's interface describes its visible characteristics. *Visible* here means usable by something (an application or object) external to the object. The notion of interface–implementation separation is essential to the fundamental object concept of encapsulation. No application or other object can directly access the implementation of an object. All access must be through the interface. This separation of interface and implementation is important to enable implementation details of an object to change without affecting other objects that use the object.

A chapter in ODMG-93 defines the basic semantic elements that can be used in defining object interfaces; these semantic elements comprise the ODMG Object Model. Another chapter defines a language called Object Definition Language (ODL) for writing object interfaces in terms that an ODMG-compliant object DBMS can implement through its bindings to C++ or Smalltalk. The object DBMSs that use C++ or Smalltalk directly for schema definition do not achieve separation of interface and implementation. The interface specification is also the implementation specification. Object DBMSs that support ODL do achieve a degree of the desired separation.

The basic semantic elements of the ODMG object model are

- The fundamental modeling primitive is the object. The terms *object* and *instance* are used interchangeably.

- Every object is uniquely identifiable by an *object identifier* (also known as an *Object_id*) that is unchangeable for the lifetime of the object.

- Objects are categorized into a hierarchy of *types* and *subtypes*. All objects of a given type have common *characteristics* of *state* and *behavior*. A subtype inherits the characteristics of its supertype(s).

- State is defined by the values objects carry for a set of *properties*. These properties can be either *attributes* of an object or *relationships* between the object and one or more other objects.

- Behavior is defined by the set of *operations* that can be applied to an object.

Not all object models have these semantics. For example, C++ defines an object as a "region of storage" [Marg90]. This is an implementation view of an object. By contrast, the ODMG object model defines an object as an abstraction, which can be implemented in a variety of ways. Unlike the implementation-level data structures and methods of a C++ class definition, the properties and operations of the ODMG object model are interface specifications. When an ODMG object model is "bound to" C++ for implementation, the properties and operations are represented as C++ data structures and methods, respectively. The ODMG object model and the object models of the object programming languages are different, but must work together.

C++ HAS ITS OWN OBJECT MODEL

Let's first consider some fundamentals of C++'s object model. An object is an instance of a class. A programmer defines a class by specifying its data elements (each with a name and type) and its member functions (each with a name, the types of its arguments, and its return type). C++ supports subclassing, a predefined set of simple data types (e.g., `char`, `int`, `short`, `long`, `float`, `double`), a predefined set of structure types (e.g., `array`), and the ability for users to define new classes that are aggregates of data elements and their operations.

C++ is sometimes referred to as a "strongly typed" language. Every

C++ variable is defined to be of a particular type. The C++ compiler checks all value assignments to ensure that the values are correctly matched to the types of the designated variables. Type checking is considered to be an attractive characteristic of C++ because the checking prevents certain kinds of errors. When a mismatch occurs, the compiler either applies a type conversion rule to force the value into a correct type, or flags the statement.

Real-world constraints determine the appropriate types for variables. Examples of these constraints include the following:

- The `iterator` variable should be of type `int`, because iterations are counted in whole number increments only.

- The `document_title` variable should be of type `string`, because document names consist of text strings.

- The `salary` variable should contain a numeric value because this kind of compensation is measured using numbers and computation using the variable must be possible.

- The `employee` object should have the data elements and member functions defined for the `Employee` class, because from the C++ point of view that is what it means to be an employee.

Each constraint is determined by the meaning—that is, the semantics—of the variable or object. Violation of a constraint could lead to errors and failure of the program. The attractiveness of strong typing is based on the assumption that the more the "system" can enforce semantics, the more likely it is that programs will work as intended. A corollary benefit is that the more the "system" can enforce semantics, the less logic the developer has to build into program code. And "less logic" implies "simpler programs," which implies "more productive programmers," which implies "software gets to market more quickly," which is good.

THE ODMG OBJECT MODEL DISTINGUISHES BETWEEN CHANGEABLE AND CONSTANT OBJECTS

Let's consider now details of some aspects of the ODMG object model. All objects have characteristics of behavior and state. Behavior is defined by the set of operations that can be applied to the object. State is defined by the values that the object has for a set of properties. These properties can be either attributes of the object or relationships between the object and one or more other objects. We'll discuss these characteristics of objects later in the chapter.

There are two basic kinds of objects: mutable and immutable. *Mutable* simply means changeable; *immutable* means constant and unchangeable. The values of a mutable object's properties may change, but an immutable object's properties can never change. Immutable objects are commonly called "literals," and mutable objects are simply called "objects." Both mutable and immutable objects have all the characteristics of objects: unique identity, type, state, behavior, and so on. In keeping with this convention, the term *denotable object* is used when it's necessary to use a single term to refer to both types of objects. The adjective *denotable* is used in the sense of objects being identifiable or distinguishable.

Mutability is an important semantic constraint. If the object DBMS knows that a particular object is immutable, it can prohibit any application from making changes to that object. For example, an object that is the set of the 50 state abbreviation codes is immutable. Applications should not change these abbreviations. Knowledge of mutability can also be important in determining the most appropriate implementation strategy for an object. For example, object programming languages typically implement literals somewhat differently than mutable objects.

ALL OBJECTS HAVE UNIQUE IDENTITY

All denotable objects have a unique immutable identity. Each object has a separate existence and can be distinguished from all other objects. When an object is created, the "system" assigns it an object identifer, commonly referred to as its *Object_id*. The object DBMS uses an object identifier to identify an object uniquely and to test equality of objects. Two objects are the same if and only if they have the same object identifier value.

Not all object models include this notion of equality based on object identifiers. For example, the OMG CORBA's core object model [Sole92] includes a notion of object identity. An object is permitted to have different object identifiers (called *objrefs*) in different contexts, and the same objref may apply to different objects, as long as they exist in different contexts. This approach simplifies the task of dealing with uniqueness in large, distributed environments.

THERE ARE MANY WAYS TO IMPLEMENT OBJECT IDENTIFIERS

The physical representation of object identifiers is not prescribed by the object model. Object DBMSs that implement the object model choose their own implementation strategies. An object DBMS may use different approaches for representing the object identifiers of objects and literals. A literal's object identifier is usually represented by the bit pattern encoding the literal's value, while a mutable object's identifier is represented by a unique bit pattern generated solely for that purpose.

Because there are many ways to implement object identifiers, it can be difficult for software packages from multiple vendors to share objects. For example, if two object DBMSs use different schemes for representing object identifiers, neither can access objects in databases created by the other, unless some translation technique is available.

C++ also has an abstract notion of identity, but it uses different representation techniques than does an object DBMS. C++ objects are all transient, meaning that their lifetimes never extend past the period of execution of the run unit, and are sometimes even shorter. In C++ a mutable object's identity is represented by its address. These addresses are used as pointer values, enabling one object to reference another in memory. C++ manages the memory space, and each object retains its identity.

Like an object DBMS, C++ treats object identifiers for mutable and immutable objects differently. A C++ literal's identity is the encoding of its value, rather than its address.

OBJECT IDENTIFIERS FOR PERSISTENT OBJECTS MUST BE LOCATION-INDEPENDENT

C++ and an object DBMS have somewhat different requirements for representing object identifiers, because they deal with objects of different lifetimes. An object DBMS cannot use main-memory addresses to represent object identity, because these addresses are too narrow in scope to accommodate persistence and distribution. Persistent objects may be stored on multiple-disk volumes residing on multiple sites of a network. An application can be scalable over time only if the objects it needs can be moved on storage and reallocated to different nodes. Just because an object is moved from one physical location to another does not alter the fact that it is the same object, and thus must retain a single object identifier.

Like object DBMS object identifiers, CORBA objrefs are unique within a network-wide scope. CORBA objrefs are assigned by an object request broker (ORB) and apply to any objects registered with the ORB. This means that objrefs can be unique, even across products from multiple vendors. In contrast, the object identifiers assigned by object DBMS products are unique only within a given vendor's product installation. Some object DBMS vendors intend to interface with ORBs to get broader scope for object identity, which may facilitate multivendor object database interoperability.

OBJECTS MAY BE ASSIGNED NAMES

An object may be given one or more application-meaningful names in addition to its object identifier. A name is a string-valued literal that can be used by the object DBMS to look up an object. These names make it easy for an application to request access to a particular object of interest. For example, an object that represents the geometry of Part #123 might be named "Part_123_Geometry". An object that represents document number X3H7-93-007v3 might be named "X3H7-93-007v3". That same object might also be named "X3H7 Object Model Features Matrix". The application determines the appropriate name to use.

Object names are not the same as primary keys in the relational model. They differ in both scope and mutability. A relational primary key is a set of columns of a table, the values of which uniquely identify rows in the table. The scope of uniqueness of a primary key is the table on which it is defined. Using a primary key to look up a row requires knowing which table the row is in. Primary keys are not mutable—if a value participating in the primary key of a row changes, the DBMS and applications consider the row to be a different row. An object, however, can be assigned new names, and its names can be changed without changing the identity or existence of the object.

The assignment of meaningful names to objects is an application responsibility. The object DBMS provides the capability to assign names and can locate objects given their names, but it does not prevent an application from changing a name on which some other application relies. The object DBMS essentially provides a name-based directory service for applications to use for their own purposes.

In ODMG-93 there is a single flat name space in a database, and a database is simply a logical collection of objects. The notions of a hierarchy or lattice of name spaces, or of name spaces that span databases, may be incorporated in a future release of the object model. This will probably be done in a way that is compatible with the naming services being adopted as part of the OMG Object Services [Sole92]. It is increasingly accepted that universal, flat scopes are difficult to manage effectively in distributed computing environments.

AN OBJECT HAS CHARACTERISTICS: PROPERTIES AND OPERATIONS

The characteristics of an object are a set of properties and operations. These characteristics are precisely what is described by the object's interface:

1. the attributes for which applications can get and/or set values

2. the relationships that applications can traverse from this object to others

3. the operations that applications can apply to this object.

Much of the rest of this chapter is devoted to discussion of object characteristics.

Some other object models, such as the OMG CORBA core object model and Smalltalk, include only operations in an object's interface. The ODMG object model includes both properties and operations, in part because of the influence of legacy database technology, which was at the other extreme and incorporated only properties and no operations in the traditional database models.

For example, consider a person object. Three characteristics of this object are name, height, and age. The ODMG object model would consider name, height, and age to be attributes (i.e., properties) of type Person. In contrast, the OMG CORBA core object model would consider name, height, and age to be operations defined as part of the interface to objects of type Person. The ODMG object model leaves open to the implementation binding details such as whether the name, height, and age attributes are represented as data fields or as functions applied to other values (e.g., birthdate) stored in the internal state of the object.

A TYPE IS A TEMPLATE FOR OBJECTS

All objects with the same interface are said to be of the same type. The definition of the type includes the specification of that interface, meaning the set of characteristics that apply to all instances. If two objects Circle_1 and Circle_2 both are of type Circle, then they have the same properties (e.g., center_x_y_coordinates, radius) and the same operations (e.g., create, draw, translate, delete). A type is like a template for objects.

Maintaining and managing information about the types in a system is the responsibility of a type manager. A strongly typed object programming language includes a type manager component, as does an object DBMS. The object DBMS's type manager works closely with the object programming language's type manager. This cooperation is necessary for the database and language environments to achieve seamless integration by sharing the type system.

In the ODMG object model, an object is typed when it is created and cannot change its type later. This constraint is consistent with C++'s object model and current object DBMS product capabilities.

CLASSES DEFINE OBJECT IMPLEMENTATIONS

An object's characteristics are insufficient to specify how it is implemented. For example, a type interface does not specify any mappings to storage structures. To allow objects to be created (also termed "instantiated"), the developer must augment a type's interface by at least one implementation specification. An implementation defines the data structures for physical representation of the instances of the type and the code for methods that operate on those data structures. For example, when an ODMG object model is bound to C++, type properties and operations are represented in C++ as data elements and member functions.

The combination of the type interface specification and one of the implementations defined for the type is called a *class*. There can be multiple implementations of a type, and those multiple classes may coexist. For example, there could be more than one class implementing an Index type: a `Hash_Table_Index` class and a `BTree_Index` class. Each has its own implementation of the abstract properties and operations of an index. There could be more than one class implementing an Invoice type: one written in C++ and the other in Smalltalk. Implementations may differ due to compiler options, or use of different algorithms, or various optimization techniques, and so forth.

The terms *type* and *class* are sometimes used interchangeably, but it is useful to be precise and use them carefully. The distinction between interface and implementation is important to support multiple implementations for a given type. As object technology becomes more pervasive, some organizations will increasingly need this distinction. They will want to be able to access the same objects from both C++ and Smalltalk, or other object programming languages. They will want to be able to use the same interface, regardless of implementation details.

In the ODMG object model, an object can belong to only one class and cannot change its class. Additionally, a type can have only one class. A future release of the model may relax these constraints and allow an object to belong to multiple classes and to change classes while retaining its type. However, most object DBMS products do not currently support these capabilities.

A TYPE CAN BE USED TO DEFINE OTHER TYPES

One of the important characteristics of an object environment is the extensibility of the type system. This means that a developer can use a type to define other types, which are called its subtypes. The original type then takes on the role of supertype for these new types. The interface of each subtype includes its supertype's interfaces. The interfaces of a type are said to be inherited by all of its subtypes. For example, Hourly_Employee is a subtype of Employee. All characteristics of Employee are inherited by Hourly_Employee. This means that an Hourly_Employee object has all the same attributes, relationships, and operations as an Employee object.

A subtype may introduce additional characteristics (i.e., attributes, relationships, and operations) that are not part of the supertype's specification. For example, the Hourly_Employee type might add an overtime_rate characteristic as part of its interface. The Retired_Employee type might add retirement_date and monthly_retirement_benefit as part of its interface. Rather than redefining the generic characteristics repeatedly for all kinds of employees (e.g., for Salaried_Employee, Retired_Employee, and Hourly_Employee), the developer can define the shared characteristics once for the supertype Employee. The developer can then reuse both the abstract specification and its implementation across all of Employee's subtypes.

Each object is considered to be an instance of an immediate type and of all that type's supertypes. The object's immediate type is its type that has no subtypes. For example, if Hourly_Employee is a subtype of Employee, and Employee is a subtype of Person, then an Hourly_Employee object is an instance of the following types: Hourly_Employee, Employee, and Person. The object has all the characteristics of all its types.

The ODMG object model is like the C++ object model, in that it supports type graphs, as opposed to strict hierarchies, so that a type may have multiple supertypes. Such a type graph is said to include multiple inheritance. An application object model can be restricted to being a strict hierarchy for object DBMS binding to programming languages, like Smalltalk, that support only single inheritance. Then no type can have more than one supertype.

A SUBTYPE CAN BE SUBSTITUTED FOR ITS SUPERTYPE

A subtype can be substituted for the supertype in any context where the supertype is valid. For example, if get_name, set_phoneNo, and get_paycheck_amount were defined on the Employee type, then they could be applied to any instance of Hourly_Employee, Salaried_Employee, or Retired_Employee. If rotate were defined on the Geometric_Figure type, then it could be applied to instances of any subtype of Geometric_Figure, such as Circle, Square, Triangle. Each of these subtypes could have its own implementation of the rotate operation, which would provide the correct behavior for the particular type of figure. This sharing of a common interface, for instance, responding to a `rotate` message, by different implementations is called *polymorphism*. Because of polymorphism, an application can invoke rotation of geometric figures, without distinction for the specific type of figure that may actually be involved at runtime.

The substitutability of subtypes for supertypes is an important factor in improving code readability, maintainability, and extensibility. Rather than hard-coding potentially large case statements or nested if-then-else structures, the application developer can code for the generic case because the object programming language environment will determine at runtime exactly which method code to invoke, depending on the kind of object that is sent a message.

TYPES HAVE PROPERTIES

Types are objects themselves; they may have attributes and participate in relationships. The attributes that the ODMG object model defines for a type are its extent's name and its uniqueness constraints. These are properties that apply to the type as a whole, rather than to individual instances of the type. The only relationships that a type has in ODMG-93 are specified by the type–subtype graph. In the future, other kinds of intertype relationships may be defined.

The set of all instances of a type is called its *extent*. The name of an extent is generally the plural form of the type's noun name—courses for the Course type, employees for the Employee type, people for the Person type. Some object DBMSs may be able to generate default extent names; some enable type definers to specify their own names.

A common use of extents is to support queries. For example, finding the identification numbers of all sailboats registered in the San Francisco Bay area involves accessing the extent containing all sailboat instances. It is the responsibility of the object DBMS to maintain extents and any indices it implements on extents. An instance is added to an extent by the object DBMS when an application creates the instance and is removed from the extent by the object DBMS when an application deletes the instance. To prevent accidental damage to the integrity of extents, an object DBMS prevents applications from accessing extents directly.

A type may have one or more uniqueness constraints, which are called *keys*. A key is one or more attributes whose values are sufficient to uniquely identify objects within the type extent. Because the scope of uniqueness is the type extent, type keys are analogous to primary keys in the relational database model. An example key for the Employee type is social_security_number. An example key for the Flight_Segment type is the combination of airline_name, from_city, to_city, and scheduled_departure_time attributes. Typically an object DBMS will automatically create and maintain indices for keys, and will use those indices to ensure that the uniqueness constraint is met when applications add objects to extents.

TYPES AND OBJECTS CAN BE ORGANIZED IN SEVERAL WAYS

One way to organize types is by their type–subtype relationships. This technique shows the inheritance structures among the types. There are other ways to organize types and objects. One approach introduced early in this chapter is to partition objects into two categories: mutable and immutable. Another approach is to partition objects by whether they are atomic or structured. An atomic object cannot be subdivided; it has no addressable constituents. A structured object can be subdivided, and its constituents can be used separately.

There are two fundamental kinds of structured objects: *structures* and *collections*. A structure can have heterogeneous elements, that is, its elements can be of more than one type. A collection must have homogeneous elements; its elements must all be of the same type. For example, all the elements of a collection object might be of type Date or of type Person.

A structure has a fixed number of named slots, each of which is typed. A slot may contain an object or a literal. That is, a structure may contain elements that are mutable or immutable and that are themselves atomic or structured. In a binding of the ODMG object model to C++ or Smalltalk, insertion and removal of objects in the slots of an object of type Structure is done by referring to these slots by name, e.g., `address.zip_code = 12345`. The literal 12345 is assigned to the literal-valued slot named `zip_code` in the structure object named `address`.

A collection, by contrast, can contain an arbitrary number of elements. The slots are not named and all elements must be of the same type. The predefined types of collections in the object model are Set, Bag, List, and Array. Arrays are one-dimensional and have varying length. The object model includes specification of the operations that are defined on each of the types. The types differ from each other in their characteristics of ordering and handling of duplicates. The predefined types are important because any object DBMS that conforms to the ODMG-93 specification is expected to implement them. Applications constructed using these types can be assured support from a variety of object DBMS products. The following table summarizes the characteristics of structures and collections.

Type name	All elements the same?	Elements ordered?	How?	Duplicates allowed?
Structure	No			
Collection	Yes			
Set	Yes	No		No
Bag	Yes	No		Yes
List	Yes	Yes	By insertion	No
Array	Yes			Yes

LITERALS CAN ALSO BE ATOMIC OR STRUCTURED

Being atomic or structured is a categorization that applies to literals as well as mutable objects. The atomic literals are the ones that usually come to mind as literals. The subtypes of Atomic_Literal in the object model are Integer, Float, Boolean, and Character. There is no explicit create operation defined on atomic literals, because all their instances implicitly preexist.

Structured literals are less intuitively understood. Structured literals enable a developer to specify that a Set, Bag, List, Array, Date, Time, or other structure is immutable. Once its values are set, they cannot be changed. For example, a person's birthdate and finger-print pattern are immutable. By contrast, all C++ literals are always atomic; they have no separable constituents. Example C++ literal constants are 14, 3.141596, 'q', 5.3E-4, and 25643UL. Example C++ string literal constants are "string", "object model", and "0123456789".

ATTRIBUTES ARE LITERAL-VALUED

Now let's consider in more detail the characteristics of objects as defined in their type interfaces: their properties and operations. The beginning of this chapter introduced the two kinds of properties: attributes and relationships. An attribute value applies to a given instance of the type, while a relationship is a property relating an instance of the type to another object, possibly of a different type. An attribute takes as its value a literal or set of literals, and does not have an object identifier. Because it does not have an object identifier, an attribute cannot be referenced by another object or an application. All access to an attribute must be via its containing object.

An attribute defines abstract state and is therefore part of the interface definition of an object type rather than its implementation. Attributes are eventually implemented according to the developer's mapping to constructs that an object programming language supports directly. This mapping is also important to the runtime object DBMS, which shares the type system of the host object programming language.

An attribute's properties are its name and the type of its legal values. The type Person might contain attribute definitions for name, age, sex, and address. The values of age and sex are probably atomic literals, while the values of name and address may be structured literals. An object DBMS might generate `set` and `get` operations in the type's implementation for each attribute defined in the type interface. For example, the `Person` C++ class, implementing the Person type, might start with the following member functions: `set_name`, `set_age`, `set_sex`, `set_address`, `get_name`, `get_age`, `get_sex`, and `get_address`.

There is no implication that an attribute must be implemented as an atomic field in a data structure. An ordered_items attribute of an invoice object might be implemented in a variety of ways: as a list of pointers to item objects, as a set of character strings containing item numbers, or as an array of references to item objects. Some attributes may be implemented in C++ as member functions. For example, `get_age` might derive an age value from a calculation using `date_of_birth` and the current date. The attribute pay_amount might be implemented by a function that calculates a value based on private data members `hours` and `hourly_rate`.

A RELATIONSHIP INVOLVES AT LEAST TWO OBJECTS

The second kind of characteristic of an object type is its relationships. Relationships are defined on types but are not type-level properties, because it is the type's instances that participate in the relationships, not the type itself. Any object may participate in relationships with other objects.

Relationships in the ODMG object model are not the same as pointers, even though a pointer also goes from one object to another. A relationship is an abstraction representing an association between objects, while a pointer is a physical construct.

A relationship is modeled by a pair of relationship signatures, each defining the type of the other object(s) involved in the relationship and the name of a traversal path used to refer to the related objects. For example (see Fig. 6-1), a student takes a set of courses, and a course is_taken_by a set of students.

The traversal path names are declared within the interface definitions of the object types participating in the relationship. The *takes* traversal path would be defined in the interface specification for the Student type; the *is_taken_by* traversal path would be defined in the interface specification for the Course type. These traversal paths are declared as inverses of each other. Traversal path cardinality is included in the specification of the target of a traversal path.

For example, using the ODMG Object Definition Language (ODL):

```
interface Student
(   extent students)
{   attribute String name;
    attribute Short student_id;
    relationship Set<Course> takes inverse Course::is_taken_by;
}
interface Course ()
{   attribute String name;
    relationship Set<Student> is_taken_by inverseStudent::takes;
}
```

FIGURE 6-1.

RELATIONSHIP BETWEEN STUDENT AND COURSE TYPES.

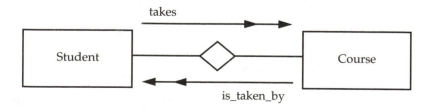

The object DBMS provides the following operations, among others, for manipulating relationships:

- **set**, which establishes a one-to-one relationship between a pair of objects. Establishing the relationship means creating the pair of traversal paths between the objects.

- **clear**, which destroys a one-to-one relationship between a pair of objects. Destroying the relationship means deleting the pair of traversal paths between the objects.

- **insert_element**, which applies only to one-to-*n* and *n*-to-*m* relationships. Adding an element means adding a pair of traversal paths.

- **remove_element**, which applies only to one-to-*n* and *n*-to-*m* relationships. Removing an element means deleting a pair of traversal paths.

- **get**, which returns a reference to a single object in the case of a one-to-one relationship or if traversing a one-to-*n* relationship from the *n*-side to the 1-side. **traverse** returns a reference to a set of objects in the case of traversing an *n*-to-*m* relationship or a one-to-*n* relationship from the 1-side to the *n*-side. The programmer may then iterate over the set to obtain the individual objects.

- **create_iterator**, which returns an iterator used by the programmer to iterate over the set of objects returned by a path traversal.

The application specifies the action to be taken; for example:

```
s->takes.insert_element(CSC531);
```

adds csc531 to the set of courses being taken by the student s. An alternative way to achieve the same outcome is simply:

```
s->takes = CSC531;
```

The object DBMS not only sets up the traversal path from student s to course csc531, but also sets up the inverse is_taken_by path.

TRAVERSAL PATHS ARE NOT THE SAME
AS POINTERS OR FOREIGN KEYS

Traversal paths are not the same as C++ pointers. First, an object DBMS creates and deletes traversal paths in pairs. In contrast, just because one C++ object points to another does not mean there is a reverse pointer. Second, it is the responsibility of an object DBMS to maintain the referential integrity of relationships. If an object that participates in a relationship is deleted, a subsequent attempt to traverse the relationship (in either direction) should raise an exception rather than referencing invalid space. For example, consider a collection of objects representing a publisher's signed book projects. If for some reason a project ends without producing a book, the relationship between that book and the publisher must be deleted. Removing the book implies adjusting the implementation of the publisher object so that it references neither the nonexistent book nor garbage. C++ associates no semantics with following a pointer. An application is allowed to dereference any of its pointers, regardless of whether they point to meaningful space.

An object DBMS cannot even use pointers directly to represent relationships, because by definition pointers are not location-independent. Because relationships are logical, they must remain valid even when the associated objects move. When an object is moved in memory, its address changes. A pointer to that object now points to something else. However, when an object is moved in memory, all of its *relationships* must retain their validity. This must be true, even if the object is moved from main memory to disk, or to a different disk volume, or to a different site on the network. Object identifiers, which are location-independent, were introduced in this chapter as the technique used by object DBMSs to represent object identity. An object DBMS can also use object identifiers to implement relationships.

Relationships have been acknowledged by the database research literature (e.g., [Hamm78] and [Smit77]) for many years, but they were not incorporated formally into the relational model until the SQL92 specification [ANSI92]. An SQL developer defines relationship traversal paths using the REFERENCES clause. REFERENCES may be implemented by foreign keys, which can have significant negative performance implications if the relational DBMS constructs the reference paths at runtime by joins.

SIDEBAR: RELATIONSHIP NAMES ARE IMPORTANT

As the ODMG object model evolves, it is likely that relationships will become first-class types. As such, they will be named and have their own properties. Relationships have names in some data modeling and object modeling techniques. These names are important in conveying the meaning of the relationships. Usually people give relationships names that are either verbs or nouns, not adjectives, or adverbs. An object DBMS really does not care how relationships are named, but it is generally less confusing to humans if the names are meaningful.

The verb-naming approach is typically used by modelers who want to construct sentences from the type–relationship–type structure. For example:

- Professor advises students.

- Employees are covered by benefit plan.

A basic difficulty with this approach is that sensible naming depends on the order of the participating types in the sentence. The example relationships could just as well have been stated:

- Student is advised by professor.

- Benefit plan covers employees.

Some diagrammatic modeling notations approach this issue by allowing for dual relationship names on diagrams. In our examples, relationship names might be advises/is_advised_by, and covers/is_covered_by. Note that being able to construct sentences (sometimes also called "business rules") using this approach still depends on using the correct type at the correct position.

When cardinalities are included, the dual-naming approach can be convenient for matching relationships with business rules. For example:

- Each professor advises no more than a dozen students, and each student is advised by one and only one professor.

- Each employee is covered by at least one benefit plan, and each benefit plan covers many employees.

Other modelers give relationships noun names. Any verb can be expressed in a noun form. For example:

- Advising—relates professors and students.
- Coverage—relates benefit plans and employees.

The noun-naming approach does not fit as well with attempts to automatically phrase business rules, but it is perhaps better suited to treatment of relationships as types themselves.

Traversal Path Names Are Also Important

The ODMG object model names the traversal paths that support associating one participating object in a relationship with another. There are several workable approaches to naming relationships. One approach is to give the traversal paths dual verb names. This approach typically implies that the relationships will get noun names. For example:

- The advising relationship between professor and student: the traversal path from professor to student could be named advises and the inverse path could be named is_advised_by.

- The coverage relationship between benefit plan and employee: the traversal path from benefit plan to employee could be named pays_for and the inverse path could be named is_covered_by.

Another approach is to give the traversal paths role-names. A role-name is a noun, giving the role of the type in the relationship. For example:

- In the advising relationship between professor and student, the professor is the advisor and the student is the advisee. Traversing the relationship from professor to student locates the professor's advisees. Traversing the relationship from student to professor finds the student's advisor.

• In the coverage relationship between benefit plan and employee, the employee is the benefactor and the benefit plan is the payor. Traversing the benefactor path from benefit plan to employee locates the benefit plan's benefactors. Traversing the path the other direction locates an employee's payor.

TYPE INTERFACES ALSO SPECIFY BEHAVIOR

The third kind of characteristic of an object type is its behavior, that is, the set of operations that can be applied to instances of the type. Each operation is modeled by its signature, which specifies the name of the operation, the name and type of each of its arguments, the name and type of any returned values, and the exceptions (i.e., error conditions) that the operation can raise. The operation's signature is specified in the type interface.

Objects interact with each other by sending messages asking for the execution of particular operations. A message contains an operation name and the identifier of the target object. Message routing and operation selection are performed at runtime, because the type of the target object may not be known at compile time. When an object is requesting another object to do something, it is acting as a client. When an object is responding to another object's request, it is acting as a server. This mode of interaction brings notions of client–server computing to the software component level.

An operation in the ODMG object model is always defined on a single object type. The object model includes no notion of an operation independent of an object type, or of an operation defined on multiple object types. Operation names need be unique only within a single type definition. Operations with the same name defined on different types are called *overloaded operations*. When an overloaded operation is invoked, a specific operation is selected for execution based on the type of the object supplied as the first argument of the actual call.

The ODMG object model does not distinguish a subcategory of operation that is free of side effects. It also does not attempt to specify the semantics of an operation. The object model assumes sequential execution of operations and does not require support for remote operations. However, it does not preclude an object DBMS from providing support for concurrent, parallel, or remote operations.

THE ODMG OBJECT MODEL IS MORE GENERAL THAN THE RELATIONAL MODEL

The ODMG object model is a superset of the relational database model as implemented in relational DBMS products today. The relational model's type hierarchy is shown in Fig. 6-2. The two roots are literal and characteristic. Entries in table columns must be literals. A literal may have an atomic (e.g., type CHARACTER) or structured (e.g., type DATE) value. The properties of the characteristics describe tables and the operations that are defined on them.

An important difference between the relational model and the ODMG object model is that the relational model does not support user-defined subtyping of the type hierarchy. Only built-in types can be used by applications. An object programmer must translate objects into the predefined structures supported by a relational DBMS in order to use the relational DBMS for persistent storage. Only the predefined, table-oriented operations supplied by SQL can be used to access the relational database. By contrast, the ODMG object model provides a way for application semantics to be expressed explicitly in the schema and supported directly by the object DBMS. Relationships in the relational model are defined as referential integrity constraints on tables and there is no concept of traversal paths.

There have been claims (e.g., [Date93] and [Pasc93]) that the relational model as originally conceived is as powerful semantically as an object

FIGURE 6-2.
RELATIONAL MODEL'S TYPE HIERARCHY.

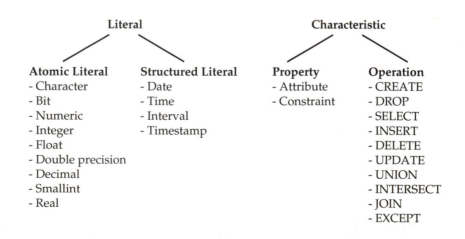

Literal		Characteristic	
Atomic Literal	**Structured Literal**	**Property**	**Operation**
- Character	- Date	- Attribute	- CREATE
- Bit	- Time	- Constraint	- DROP
- Numeric	- Interval		- SELECT
- Integer	- Timestamp		- INSERT
- Float			- DELETE
- Double precision			- UPDATE
- Decimal			- UNION
- Smallint			- INTERSECT
- Real			- JOIN
			- EXCEPT

model. These claims are based on equating the relational notion of domain with the object notion of type. By allowing a relational table to include a rich set of domains, rather than the relatively restricted set of built-in types offered by most relational DBMSs today, the ability of relational databases to handle more kinds of data would certainly be enhanced. However, these domains need to be able to be extensible by application type definers. The domain notion also needs to be enhanced with the ability to specify operations. Note that most object DBMS products today do little with operations either.

THERE ARE OTHER OBJECT DBMS MODELS

Not all object DBMSs implement these notions of the ODMG object model, with its abstract attributes, relationships, and operations. For example, some object DBMSs (e.g., [Daya89] and [Fish87]) use a somewhat simpler, but powerful, model with roots in the functional model [Ship81]. In this model, all characteristics of objects are functions. State information is accessed via `get` and `set` functions. A `get` function applied to an object may return a value, which is the last value that a corresponding `set` function made current. For example, a `get_salary` function returns the last value that resulted from application of the `set_salary` function. A `get_advisor` function returns the professor object representing this object's advisor.

The functional model is also the basis of the OMG core object model [Sole92], as well as the Smalltalk model. All state information is encapsulated by methods and is accessible only through method invocation.

The ODMG object model includes attributes and relationships in part because object DBMS technology has roots in the entity–relationship and semantic data modeling technologies. In fact, most object DBMS products today place significantly more emphasis on the data side of objects than on their operations. Perhaps when the ODMG object model includes more comprehensive specification of operations, the functional and data-oriented models will converge.

AN OBJECT MODEL CAN BE USED WITH A NONOBJECT IMPLEMENTATION

The ODMG object model could be used in development of an application that is implemented using a relational DBMS. However, because a relational DBMS does not support all the semantic constructs of the object model, some of the information captured in the model will necessarily be lost in the relational database. If these "lost" semantics are to be enforced, their logic must be encoded in application programs (see Fig. 6-3).

The ODMG object model could also be used in development of applications that do not require any database support at all. However, because the ODMG object model captures more semantics than do the object programming languages, such as C++ and Smalltalk, the developer may need to program some object model semantics into application code.

IN CLOSING . . .

An object DBMS's object model is important, because it determines the built-in semantics that the product understands and can enforce. Any semantics that can be enforced by the environment, such as the compiler or the object DBMS, do not have to be coded into applications. The enforcement code only has to be written once, instead of left as the responsibility of any application developers who encounter the semantic situation. Being able to define abstract semantics independent of implementation can be important in achieving interoperability and portability of applications.

FIGURE 6-3.
USE OF ODMG OBJECT MODEL TO DEVELOP APPLICATION IMPLEMENTED WITH RELATIONAL TECHNOLOGY.

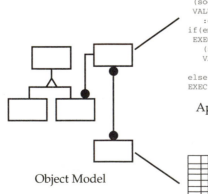

```
EXEC SQL INSERT INTO Employee_R
  (soc_no,emp_name,birth_date,dept_name)
  VALUES (:emp->socNo,:emp->name,:emp->birthDate,
    :emp->deptName);
if(emp->type==1)
  EXEC SQL INSERT INTO Student_R
    (soc_no,study_yr,degree,hourly_rate,hours)
    VALUES(:emp->socNo,:emp->studyYr,:emp->degree,
      :emp->hourlyRate,:emp->hours);
else if(emp.type==2)...
EXEC SQL COMMIT WORK RELEASE;
```

Application Code

Object Model

Relational Tables

CHAPTER 7

Storing and Finding Persistent Objects

This chapter discusses techniques that object DBMSs use to store objects and to manage the movement of objects between persistent storage and program memory. This is an area of significant operational difference between object DBMSs and previous generations of DBMS technology, primarily because an object DBMS is tightly coupled to its programming language environment. This coupling results in the illusion of single-level memory, even when some objects are in program memory, some are in local persistent storage, and some are remotely located across the network. In addition to discussing this single-level storage model, this chapter also introduces techniques for managing large volumes of objects.

Managing large volumes of data typically is not of particular concern to a programming language, but it is an important consideration for a DBMS, whether it supports an object model, relational model, or some other model. Databases range in size from being rather small (megabytes) to exceeding terabytes of storage. Today's object databases are not yet that large, but their volume requirements are expanding rapidly. Object DBMSs leverage techniques like indexing and clustering that have been used for years by network and relational DBMS products. They also introduce some new techniques.

Not all commercially available object DBMSs manage object storage the same way. This chapter introduces some representative approaches here as illustrations of how products approach object storage issues. We'll discuss:

1. memory models and client–server configurations

2. object identification and location

3. improving performance through caching, clustering, and indexing

4. object replication.

Let's turn first to a more specific discussion of the differences between the relational database two-level storage model and the object database single-level storage model.

SOME DBMSs SUPPORT TWO-LEVEL STORAGE

The conventional DBMS storage model has at least two levels: database storage in on-line secondary devices like disks and program storage in main memory or virtual memory (see Fig. 7-1). A third level may be introduced for archiving. It is appropriate to omit consideration of archive storage for now, as many of the considerations are the same for both object and relational databases.

In contrast to the storage model of conventional DBMSs, the object database on-line storage model has just one level, which unifies database and program memory. How are these two approaches different, and what are the implications?

First, the terminology itself can be confusing. We make a clear distinction here between "memory" and "storage." We use the term "memory" to refer to main memory or virtual memory. This space is directly addressable by the programming language environment. The program variables defined in C++, C, or COBOL are allocated space in memory. We use the term "storage" to refer to secondary storage devices, which provide nonvolatile storage. Storage is persistent, and objects that are allocated space in storage are persistent objects, also known as database objects.

FIGURE 7-1.
MULTILEVEL MEMORY MODEL.

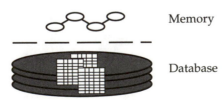

Memory

Database

The conventional database approach treats storage and memory differently. The traditional DBMS model is that the primary copy of data is on stable nonvolatile storage. Databases persist, regardless of the existence of particular application programs executing in memory. The DBMS records data updates in log files, which the DBMS applies to update data in storage as part of certain transaction commit functions. The DBMS uses transaction management and recovery techniques to keep the primary copy of all data consistent. Crash recovery includes returning the primary copy to a consistent state by traversing the log, undoing updates from incomplete transactions, and redoing transactions that have been committed but whose results have not yet been written to the primary copy.

The DBMS's responsibility is protection of databases on persistent storage, which in this model is protection of the primary copy of data. The DBMS has no responsibility for transient data, that is, for data in program memory. There is a clear, well-defined separation between database space and program space. This distinction manifests itself in several ways: perhaps most notably in the languages and models used by applications to access data in each space.

RELATIONAL DBMSs SUPPLY THEIR OWN TYPE SYSTEMS

A relational DBMS supplies its own type system and language—SQL—for accessing database storage, and the programming language is used to access program memory. (Refer to Chapter 5 for some SQL examples.) Not only does SQL have its own syntax for statement formulation, it also has its own notions of variables and operators. In addition to the basic SELECT, UPDATE, DELETE, and INSERT verbs, SQL includes GROUP BY, ORDERED BY, MIN, MAX, and AVG operators, among others. The variables used in SQL statements are SQL variables, not C++, C, or COBOL variables, with the exception of the programming language variables that are bound to SQL variables. For example:

```
SELECT AVG emp.sal
FROM Employee emp
WHERE emp.level <= :next_level;
```

Here `next_level` is a program variable, while `sal` and `level` are both database variables. The value of program variable `next_level` is compared with the database field `emp.level`. Database operators, like `AVG`, can be applied only to database fields, like `emp.sal`, not to program variables.

RELATIONAL DBMSs USE A TWO-PROCESS MODEL

Relational DBMSs typically use a two-process execution model. The DBMS runtime is isolated into its own process, separate from the application's process (see Fig. 7-2). Each interaction of the application with the DBMS requires interprocess communication. Interprocess calls (IPCs) are relatively expensive, requiring on the order of 10 milliseconds each. This is about the same as the time required for a disk access.

Let's consider the sequence of events that occur when an application reads and then updates a database record (see Fig. 7-3). Assume that the application executes a `SELECT` statement, for example, to find an employee with a specified name. To simplify the discussion, assume that only one record in the database meets the selection criterion. Assuming that the `SELECT` is not posed against a temporary table resulting from a previous query, the record is by definition on secondary storage in a database.

The sequence of events is as follows:

• The relational DBMS uses indexes or table scans to determine which page on disk contains the qualifying record.

FIGURE 7-2.
CONVENTIONAL DBMS TWO-PROCESS MODEL.

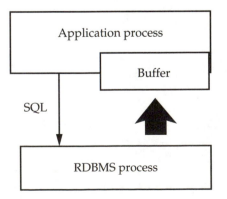

FIGURE 7-3.

ACCESSING A RECORD FROM TWO-LEVEL STORAGE.

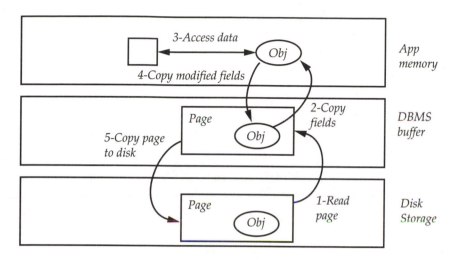

- The DBMS reads that page from disk and copies it into a page frame in its main-memory address space. The collection of page frames reserved for this purpose is called the *database buffer*. In some systems the DBMS copies only the record-of-desire into the buffer; in others the DBMS copies the entire page. To simplify things, assume entire pages are being copied.

- The application cannot address the database buffer. So, the DBMS copies fields of the database record into program variables in the application's address space, according to the binding information supplied in the SELECT statement. Some DBMSs make this transfer a field at a time; others copy in whole-record units.

- The application can now directly address the program variables and make whatever changes are appropriate.

- If the application calls for updating the database, it issues an SQL UPDATE statement. The DBMS copies values from program variables into fields of a record in the database buffer space.

- When the transaction commits, the DBMS copies the updated record back to an appropriate location in storage. This location may or may not be the same as the originating location for the record, depending on the circumstances of storage management. If it is a different location or if indexed-attribute values have been updated, then the DBMS must also update affected indexes.

An application's SELECT statement to access a record from disk into the database buffer and copy values into program variables typically requires execution of over 10,000 machine instructions. Let's see how this compares with the object database approach.

OBJECT DATABASES GIVE THE ILLUSION OF SINGLE-LEVEL MEMORY

A major objective of object databases is to simplify greatly a programmer's dealings with persistent storage by providing the illusion of single-level memory. Behind this illusion, there may actually be one or more levels of persistent storage. The programmer, however, never needs to deal directly with moving objects between levels. The basic philosophy is that it is the object DBMS's responsibility, not the programmer's responsibility, to know when persistent storage needs to be accessed. When a C++ program statement references an object, either that object is already in the program's memory space, or the object DBMS must capture the reference, determine where the pertinent object is stored, and bring it into the program's memory space. By contrast, the relational programmer needs to know when database access is required and use SQL for those accesses.

The object database illusion of single-level memory is achieved by cooperation between the language environment and the object DBMS. They share memory space that is commonly called the "object cache." Both the

FIGURE 7-4.
SINGLE-LEVEL MEMORY MODEL.

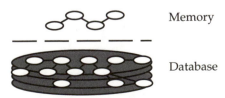

Memory

Database

language and object DBMS runtime components can address this space. The object cache appears to the programming language as another class of storage. For C++, this storage class is a subregion of heap memory. The object cache appears to the object DBMS as a buffer between secondary storage and the application.

SINGLE-LEVEL MEMORY EXTENDS VIRTUAL MEMORY

Single-level memory extends the virtual memory to include persistent storage, which may be physically local or remote. This is a natural extension to the concepts of virtual memory that have evolved over the last 20 years. In the old days, programs were confined to the space offered by real memory. However, many applications would not fit easily into these constraints, which commonly were on the order of 64K. It was the programmer's responsibility to figure out how to segment the code, so that necessary portions could be memory resident at any given time, and to coordinate overlaying these segments during execution. This was not trivial work!

In the mid-1970s, virtual memory was invented to extend memory address space past the confines of physical memory. Programs with addressing requirements that exceed the physical memory space typically

FIGURE 7-5.
SHARED OBJECT CACHE.

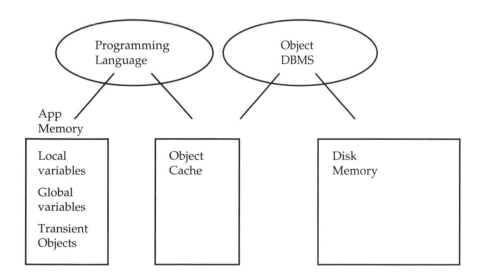

FIGURE 7-6.
VIRTUAL MEMORY ADDRESSING.

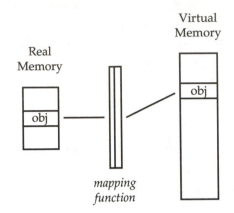

will fit within the bounds of the virtual memory space. Virtual memory is implemented with address translation techniques that allow programs to address the larger, virtual memory space in exactly the same way as they would address the physical memory. A virtual address translator maps between the virtual addresses and real addresses (see Fig. 7-6).

The virtual memory space is commonly managed using a paging tech-

FIGURE 7-7.
FETCHING A PAGE INTO REAL MEMORY.

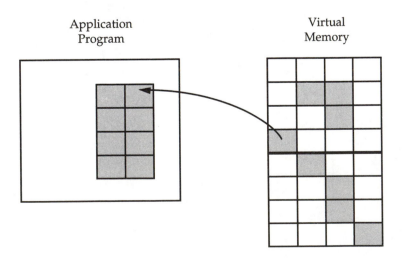

nique. The real memory (or a part of it) is partitioned into fixed-sized blocks called page frames. The virtual memory is organized into blocks called pages; the pages fit into the page frames. It is the operating system's responsibility to detect when a program is referencing a page that is not resident in a page frame of the real memory. When the operating system traps such a fault, it fetches the requested nonresident page from storage, assigns it to a page frame, and the faulting process resumes execution (see Fig. 7-7).

The size of virtual memory varies for different operating systems, but a typical system uses 32-bit addresses, giving 2**32 addressable locations. This is not enough space for many database applications. The single-level memory of an object database is the next logical step in extending virtual memory to include persistent storage (see Fig. 7-8).

The extended virtual memory space can now make use of locations that are physically resident on secondary storage, including storage devices that may be mounted at remote sites of the network. The typical system uses 64-bit addresses, which dramatically increases the capacity of the addressable

FIGURE 7-8.
EXTENDING VIRTUAL MEMORY ADDRESSING TO PERSISTENT STORAGE.

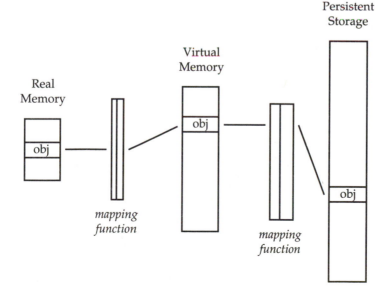

storage system. To put the difference in perspective, consider the following. If 32-bit addresses were assigned at the rate of 100 per millisecond, they would all be used in about 30 seconds. If 64-bit addresses were used at the same rate, it would take about 5000 years to use them all!

An object DBMS bears responsibility for mapping pages from secondary storage onto the operating system's virtual memory scheme. Let's see what happens when a program wants to access an object that's not currently in its memory space. Assume that the object-of-desire's identifier is its extended virtual memory address. Reference to the object will cause a page fault because the object's address is on a nonresident page.

The sequence of events shown in Fig. 7-9 is as follows:

1. The object DBMS locates the addressed page on storage and maps the page into a page frame in the application's memory space. The collection of page frames reserved for this purpose is called the *object cache*.

2. If the object contains references to other objects, the object DBMS converts those references to virtual-memory addresses, so that the application can use them as programming language pointers. This process is called *swizzling*.

FIGURE 7-9.
ACCESSING AN OBJECT FROM EXTENDED VIRTUAL MEMORY.

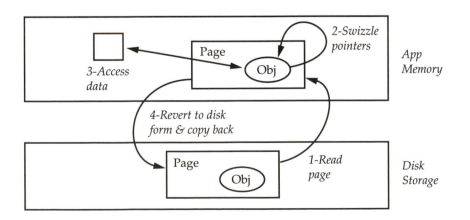

3. The application can now directly address the object and make whatever updates are appropriate.

4. When the program completes, or when the object DBMS needs to swap the page out of its page frame to make room for another page, the object DBMS converts the page containing the updated object back to its disk form and copies it to storage, replacing the original version of that page.

If the application again references the now-swapped-out object-of-desire, the faulting process occurs again, resulting in another iteration of the above sequence of events.

SINGLE-LEVEL MEMORY IMPLIES A SINGLE-PROCESS MODEL

The single-level memory model not only integrates the programming language and object database, but also can significantly affect database application performance. The object DBMS runtime is linked with the application process rather than being separated into its own process (see Fig. 7-10). Objects that have been fetched from disk are cached into address space shared by the object DBMS and the programming language.

The object DBMS and programming language share the same type system. When objects are brought into the cache, they are represented in the programming language's format. Typically the object DBMS also uses this representation on disk, although an object DBMS to support multiple programming languages might elect not to do this. Moving an object from the disk representation to the programming language representation generally requires that the object DBMS:

1. swizzle interobject references—change disk pointers to main-memory pointers

2. make minor structural changes and entries in programming language data structures, for example, record certain information in a format that C++ can use

3. convert data representations if the object comes from a server with a different machine architecture or a different compiler.

FIGURE 7-10.
OBJECT DBMS SINGLE-POCESS MODEL.

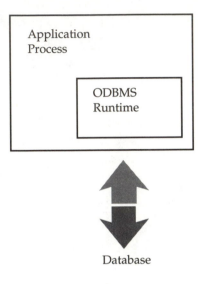

The application can then access the object directly, just as if it were a transient programming language object. Because the object DBMS and the programming language can both access objects directly once they have been fetched into the shared cache memory, the interprocess communication that would be required if separate processes were used for the object DBMS runtime and the application is avoided.

Thus, the object database has the effect of extending virtual memory to encompass disk storage. In fact, the object database extends virtual memory to encompass the network. The programmer can access objects stored anywhere in the distributed database environment using just the object programming language. The object DBMS handles finding and addressing objects regardless of whether they are local or remote.

OBJECT DBMSs SUPPORT CLIENT–SERVER CONFIGURATIONS

Object databases are commonly used in distributed computing environments. A relatively simple distributed computing configuration is a set of client desktop machines (workstations or personal computers) and a server node, interconnected by a local-area network. The desktop machines are application nodes, while the server is a database node. Object database applications are typically configured with the application code and the client part of the object DBMS runtime linked together at each client site, and the server part of the object DBMS located at the site acting as a database server (see Fig. 7-11).

The interaction between client and server components requires communication. For instance, a client may need to access an object that is stored in the server's database. This communication is typically implemented as a remote procedure call (RPC), which is even more expensive than an IPC. However, once the object DBMS has moved a persistent object from the server to the client-side object cache, no additional IPC overhead is incurred when the application accesses that object.

This architecture, which links the object DBMS runtime with the application, sometimes raises concerns for database integrity protection. This concern is typically voiced by people who are familiar with the relational architectures that keep the DBMS and application completely separate. Because the application program and the object DBMS share the same address space, there is opportunity for the application to make database changes without being subject to object DBMS controls and integrity checks. In fact, however, the strong typing of the object database is likely to catch the majority of such errors.

FIGURE 7-11.
BASIC CLIENT–SERVER CONFIGURATION.

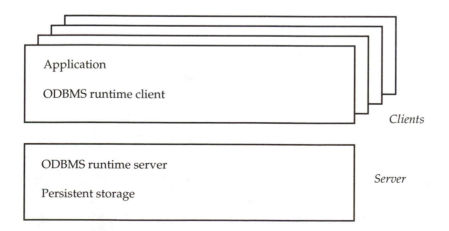

Nonetheless, some object DBMS vendors favor using the dual-process client–server configurations of their products, even when the components are located at the same site. In these cases, the server component of the object DBMS should not be linked with the process that contains the application and the client component of the object DBMS. The tradeoff, of course, is an adverse impact on performance due to interprocess communication requirements. Keeping the server process separate from the application process addresses the concern about database integrity only to the extent that the server actually performs integrity checks.

A PERSISTENT OBJECT'S IDENTIFIER IS ITS DATABASE ADDRESS

Linking the client part of the object DBMS runtime with the application requires the object DBMS to manage access to individual objects in a manner compatible with the approach taken by the object programming language. An important aspect of achieving this compatibility is the treatment of object identifiers, which are used to uniquely identify and locate objects.

Both the object DBMS and the object programming language deal with object identifiers. A persistent object's identifier is its database address. Object programming languages typically use virtual memory addresses as object identifiers. A simple approach is to equate logical object identification with physical addressing. Since no two objects can be stored at the same location, each virtual memory address is guaranteed to be a unique identifier. A reference from one object to another is implemented as a pointer, whose value is the target object's location in virtual memory. In C++ on a 32-bit machine, each object has a 32-bit object identifier, which is its location in main memory.

Using virtual memory addresses to implement object identifiers is unsatisfactory for some object databases. The resulting address space is not large enough to accommodate networked environments and distributed objects. Tying logical identification inextricably to physical addresses prevents the object DBMS from being able to move objects without significant work to find and repair all references to those objects. On the other hand, once an object has been assigned a virtual memory address, using that address as the object's identifier can deliver excellent performance.

The technique used by the object DBMS for implementation of object identifiers is a major determinant of the performance and scalability of the object database. If the implementation is "close" to virtual memory addresses, then access performance will benefit. On the other hand, if a level of indirection is introduced, then scalability will benefit. The object database will be able to gracefully handle growing populations of persistent objects in response to a wide variety of unanticipated activity.

Some object DBMSs use 64-bit addressing instead of the programming language's 32-bit scheme. One approach is to use high-order bits, say the first 16, to represent an identifying number for the birthsite of the object, and to fill the lower order bits, say the other 48, with a guaranteed-unique generated number. An alternative is to incorporate a timestamp into the object identifier when the object is created. In a distributed environment, this approach must account for potential difficulties in synchronizing time clocks across sites.

While 64-bit addressing can accommodate a large number of objects, it may not be sufficient for the needs of networked databases. Difficulties arise when two networks with previously distinct address spaces must be connected. This may happen when one organization acquires another, along with its networks, or when a wide-area link is connected into a local-area network. In these situations, a birthsite identifier may no longer be unique. Each of the two previously unconnected object database installations may have used the same starting point and algorithm for generating site identifiers. Resolving this situation may require the object DBMS to incorporate a network identifier into object identifiers.

Sometimes object representations include a header field that stores the object's type identifier. Alternatively, the object DBMS may encode type information in the object's identifier. This second approach has the benefit of enabling the object DBMS to determine the type of an object without fetching that object, with the tradeoff that significant overhead has to be carried in all object identifiers.

PERSISTENCE MAY BE INHERITED OR DEFINED AS A STORAGE CLASS

There are two major approaches to persistence implemented in commercial object DBMSs. One is through inheritance from a base class; the other is by defining persistence as a storage class at the language level. The storage class implementation is simpler from a programmer's point of view because it offers completely consistent treatment of transient and persistent objects. Single-level extended virtual memory is more easily implemented by the object DBMS when persistence is a storage class. The programmer can consider database space to be a storage scoping alternative on par with other programming-language–provided scopes (e.g., procedure and process).

The other major alternative is for the object DBMS to supply a class (called `Persistent_Object` in ODMG-93 [Catt94]) that allows the type definer to specify when a class is able to have persistent as well as transient instances. Classes derived from `Persistent_Object` are called "persistence-capable."

If an application uses a base-class object DBMS to give persistence to a preexisting C++ class library, the application developer must modify the declaration of all classes that may potentially have persistent instances to inherit from the base class. This modification requires access to the source code of the class library. If the source is not accessible, then an object DBMS that provides persistence as a C++ storage class may be more suitable, as it will not require changes to class definitions.

OBJECTS ARE ACCESSED BY DATABASE ADDRESSES

Let's turn now to techniques for accessing objects that are stored persistently in an object database. A C++ or Smalltalk program typically accesses an object by supplying its variable name, or a pointer or reference to the object. Database objects are accessed in a similar fashion by following database references or in a more conventionally database way by queries. Chapter 9 discusses queries. Here we discuss access by database references.

ODMG-93 specifies a template class `Ref`, which provides smart pointers. `Ref`s behave in many respects like C++ pointers but provide additional mechanics for guaranteeing the integrity of references to persistent objects. For example,

```
Ref <City> shipping_city;
```

declares `shipping_city` as a reference to an object of type `city`. Although the syntax for declaring a database reference is different from the syntax for declaring a C++ pointer, the usage is largely the same. For example, `Refs` may be dereferenced using the `*` operator.

An object DBMS implements a `Ref` by mapping an object identifier, which is its database address, to a physical address. Different object DBMSs use different techniques for this mapping. In any case, when one object references another, the object DBMS must locate the second object and fetch it into the cache, where it can be accessed directly by the object programming language runtime.

References between objects on disk are represented directly or indirectly by disk addresses. These addresses cannot be used by C++, which understands only virtual memory addresses. The object DBMS must change these addresses to references that can be processed by C++. *Swizzling* is a technique the object DBMS uses to change object references to main-memory pointers.

When the object DBMS fetches an object, it may swizzle all the references at once or incrementally. If the unit of transfer into the object cache is a page, then all the objects on that page must have their references swizzled. Swizzling all references at once is sometimes called *eager swizzling* [Moss90]. Not only does the object DBMS transform the references in the fetched objects to pointers, but it also traverses those references, fetches all reachable objects, and swizzles their references. The DBMS may use a table of reference-pointer pairs to resolve multiple uses of the same reference value to the same virtual memory address. The result is that after the initial fetch, access to reachable persistent objects proceeds in the same way as access to transient objects. C++ can take over from the object DBMS.

Consider persistent object A, which references persistent object B. Assume that the page containing object A is already in program memory space. The swizzling process treats each pointer on A's page, allocating and reserving a virtual memory page for the persistent-storage page containing the pointed-to object, unless the referenced page has already been mapped to virtual memory. The application now needs to dereference A's reference to B. The reference to B has already been swizzled and is now a pointer to a reserved page frame. Because the object DBMS has not yet brought in B's page to fill that frame, a page fault occurs. The object DBMS loads the page containing B into its preassigned location in memory.

The application has to deal only with virtual memory addresses, because the object DBMS reserves pages in advance for all reachable objects when it brings a page into memory. Because the application deals only with virtual memory addresses, it can handle references between all objects, transient or persistent, uniformly. The pointer operator syntax of C++ can be used directly, regardless of whether the referenced object is transient or persistent. Some object DBMSs use *lazy swizzling* and fetch objects only when they are actually referenced. This approach can be beneficial if the probability of traversing the reachable objects is relatively low. The input/output costs are incurred only when needed.

SOME OBJECT DBMSs DON'T SWIZZLE UNTIL DEREFERENCE

Both eager and lazy swizzling transform all references on a page to pointers when that page is fetched into cache memory. Eager swizzling also fetches the pages referenced by objects on the initially fetched page, while lazy swizzling does not fetch pages until the references are actually used. Another alternative is to postpone not just the page fetch, but also the swizzling, until the reference is needed. This approach maintains object references as logical object identifiers rather than virtual memory addresses, even when the objects are in the cache. One way to implement this approach is called an *object-descriptor architecture*. This architecture introduces a level of indirection between objects and the objects they reference. The object DBMS maintains a hash table of pointers to all objects that are resident in the cache (see Fig. 7-12).

The hash table is sometimes called a resident object table or a cached object table. Each entry refers indirectly to a cached object; each points directly to an object descriptor, also known as the object's *surrogate*, which then points directly to the cached object. If the object is not yet in the cache or has been swapped out of the cache, then the object descriptor may have a null pointer, indicating that the object is nonresident. A reference from one cached object to another is implemented as a pointer to the referenced object's descriptor, rather than as a pointer directly to the object.

Introducing a level of indirection gives the object DBMS considerable flexibility in moving objects and managing storage. It also means that the object DBMS can wait to resolve references until the application actually needs to use the reference. The object descriptor may include other informa-

FIGURE 7-12.
OBJECT-DESCRIPTOR ARCHITECTURE.

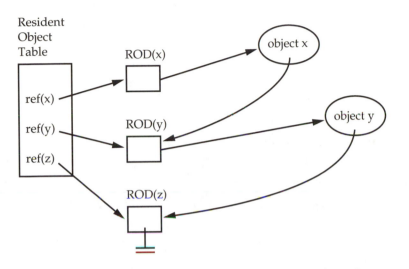

tion used by the object DBMS to manage the object, including, for example, the object's class identifier, indicators for whether the object has been modified or locked, and versioning information. If objects are small, the object descriptors can occupy a relatively large amount of memory space. However, having this information readily available at runtime can be of benefit to the object DBMS.

The object-descriptor architecture delivers slower access times to cache-resident objects than does the virtual memory mapping approach with eager or lazy swizzling. Because of the level of indirection, references cannot possibly be followed at C++ speeds. However, there is the tradeoff of not incurring costs to swizzle references that will never be followed or to fault in objects that will never be accessed. The object-descriptor architecture transfers objects between the persistent storage and the object cache, while the virtual memory mapping approach transfers pages.

Which approach delivers better performance? The answer depends on the characteristics of the application. The virtual memory mapping approach can deliver excellent performance, especially for small, well-clustered databases. The object-descriptor architecture can also deliver excellent performance, especially for large databases with a variety of application access patterns, sustained over a long period.

OBJECTS MAY BE ACCESSED VIA RELATIONSHIP TRAVERSAL PATHS

Database object references also may occur in the specification of relationship traversal paths. Chapter 6 introduced relationships as logical associations between objects. Recall that there is a formal distinction between the semantics of a relationship traversal path and those of a C++ pointer. Relationship traversal paths occur in pairs, each representing one direction of a bidirectional relationship. In contrast, a C++ pointer from an Employee object to a Department object has no implication of existence of an inverse pointer from the Department object to the Employee object.

A relationship traversal path takes as its value references to one or more objects; a pointer takes as its value an address. There are a variety of ways that an object database can implement relationship traversal paths, with accompanying tradeoffs in performance and ease of use. Consider first a simple one-to-one relationship, for example the marital relationship between spouses. This kind of relationship is typically implemented by a pair of references, one on each end of the relationship (see Fig. 7-13). In the marriage example, each Married_Person object contains a reference to another Married_Person object.

There are several ways for the object database to represent relationships that have cardinality greater than one. Consider a one-to-many advising relationship between types Professor and Student. One way to represent the advisees traversal path from a Professor object to the associated Student objects is for the object DBMS to embed in each Professor object a set of references to Student objects (see Fig. 7-14). Each Student object could have a

FIGURE 7-13.

REPRESENTATION OF A ONE-TO-ONE RELATIONSHIP.

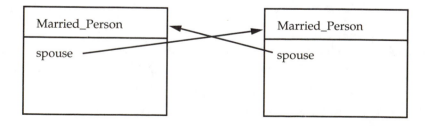

FIGURE 7-14.
REPRESENTATION OF A ONE-TO-MANY RELATIONSHIP.

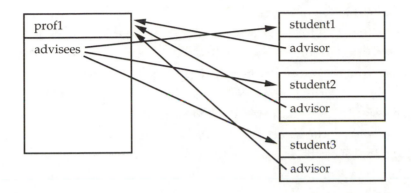

single reference to implement the inverse advisor traversal path to the appropriate Professor object.

When an application inserts an additional Student object in the advising relationship, the object DBMS must add a reference for that Student object into the advisees set in the appropriate Professor object. Additionally, the object DBMS must establish the inverse advisor traversal path in the Student object. When an application traverses the traversal path from a Professor object to find her advisees, the object DBMS dereferences all the elements in the traversal path set.

When an application removes a Student object from the advising relationship, the object DBMS removes the reference for that Student object from the advisees set in the appropriate Professor object and sets the advisor traversal path in the Student object to a null value. The object DBMS must update both traversal paths to maintain the relationship integrity and prevent dangling references. Note that this is not the semantics of C++ pointers. If an application deletes the data structure at the address referred to by a C++ pointer, it is still legal for the application to dereference that pointer. C++ returns whatever is currently at that address, regardless of whether it makes any sense to the application. In contrast, if the application deletes the object referred to by a relationship traversal path, a subsequent attempt to cross the path should cause an exception to be raised. The object DBMS should not return merely whatever object or object fragment is at the address.

The object DBMS could represent a fixed-cardinality relationship, such as one to twelve, using a fixed-size array of references. The object DBMS could then enforce the cardinality constraint on insertion of instances into the relationship.

An alternative to using a set of Student references embedded in the Professor object is for the object DBMS to store in each Professor object a reference to a set of references (see Fig. 7-15). This approach results in a somewhat simpler data management task for the object DBMS, since the variable-sized set is now represented separately from the rest of the Professor object. The object DBMS does not assign the set an object identifier, and the set can be accessed only using the traversal path.

Both transient and persistent objects may participate in relationships. However, a persistent object cannot refer at commit time to a transient object. Its reference would be to an object that probably will not exist when the first object is again accessed from persistent storage. This constraint on relationships is consistent with programming language principles. For example, in C++ an object whose lifetime is that of the process cannot safely refer to objects whose lifetime is procedure-based, because the stack frame-based storage allocated to procedure objects goes away upon procedure return. If process-life objects retained pointers to the virtual memory addresses at which those objects had been allocated originally, that storage might have been reused for something else by the time the program

FIGURE 7-15.
ANOTHER APPROACH TO REPRESENTING RELATIONSHIPS.

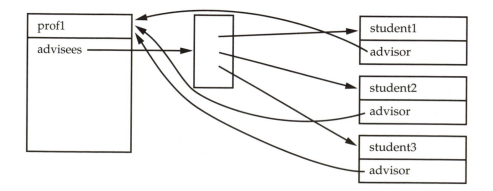

attempted to dereference those pointers. References from transient to persistent objects are always permissible.

MANY FACTORS DETERMINE PERFORMANCE

Many other storage-management factors besides pointer management and interprocess communication affect database application performance. The object programmer does not want the database to slow application execution. The C++—object DBMS combination is expected to run essentially at C++ speeds. The Smalltalk—object DBMS combination is expected to run essentially at Smalltalk speeds. This objective is, of course, impossible to achieve. Access to secondary storage will always be slower than access to main memory.

There are, however, many factors the application developer can use to keep access times as low as possible, including:

- cache sizes

- clustering

- indexes

- replication.

CACHES SHOULD ACCOMMODATE WORKING SETS

The client-side cache is the buffer space for objects to be accessed and rereferenced by the application. Database researchers long ago developed a concept that each application has a *working set*, which is the set of data the application uses in a period. Many applications have high working set locality, that is, the working set changes quite slowly after the initial load of the buffer space. If the cache is large enough to store the working set of objects, then the developer can minimize disk accesses. Disk accesses are slower than main-memory or cache accesses, so caching is good for performance.

In fact, the best possible disk-access performance will be achieved if the application accesses the disk just once. This happens if the object DBMS brings all the objects used by the application into the cache at once. There are two difficulties with this approach: knowing in advance which objects the application will use and making the cache large enough to accommodate all these objects. Some object DBMSs have facilities for applications to specify which objects they will need. For example, some object DBMSs provide facilities for an application to request access to container objects, which are comprised of other objects. The entire container of objects is transferred to the cache at once. Container objects are heavily used in some kinds of applications, for example CAD. Even before the use of object databases, CAD systems supported a model of interaction in which a user would load a file containing design information into memory, work on it there, then save modifications in a new version of the file.

For many interactive applications, however, it is impossible to predetermine which specific objects will be accessed by a particular run unit. Rather, the object DBMS must cache objects as they are requested. Faulting objects one at a time into the cache can be excessively time-consuming if many objects are required. To improve on this situation, an object DBMS may attempt to predict which other objects will be needed when a particular object is requested by an application. The eager swizzling approach introduced earlier does this prefetching by faulting in referenced objects even before the application dereferences those objects. For example, bringing a particular Student object into the cache also causes not only all the other objects on that page to be made cache-resident, but also all the objects on pages containing objects that the Student instance references. A developer using an object DBMS that does eager swizzling should ensure that caches are allocated sufficient memory space to accommodate these pages.

EFFECTIVE CLUSTERING MINIMIZES PAGE FAULTS

Object DBMSs typically use double buffering, with an object cache on the client side and a page buffer on the server side. Not only do object caches and page buffers need to be sized appropriately, the developer should also pay attention to the traffic between the disk and the page buffer (see Fig. 7-16). When a DBMS accesses an object from a disk page, it also brings all the other objects on that page into the page buffer, because the page is the unit of transfer between the disk and the page buffer. Page faulting could be minimized if other objects the application needs were stored

FIGURE 7-16.
PAGE BUFFERS AND CLIENT CACHES.

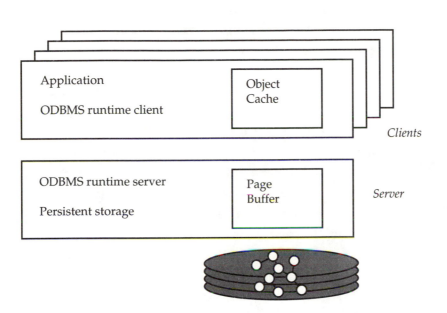

on that same page. For example, if a Student object references a Professor object, then storing those two objects on the same page would mean that there would be only one disk access required to make both objects available to the application. If they are on different pages, then two disk accesses will be needed.

Storing objects together that are highly likely to be used together is called *clustering*. Good clustering means that the object DBMS can access objects that will be used together with high probability of minimal page faulting.

If objects are not well clustered, considerable paging activity can result when an application accesses a single object. For example, consider again eager swizzling. The object DBMS will bring fewer pages into the cache if referenced objects are clustered onto the same page rather than stored on different pages. Improving object clustering can make substantial improvements in application performance.

Some object DBMSs allow the application to specify which objects should be clustered. This is typically done by enabling the programmer to indicate that an object should be stored as close as possible to another specified object, or at least in the same segment of the database. Object DBMSs implement clustering techniques that accommodate compound, variable-length objects (e.g., [Chen91], [Tsan92]).

Some object DBMSs support clustering by class. These object DBMSs attempt to store all instances of a given class together. Class-based clustering typically is not appropriate for applications that need to traverse relationships between objects, for example, from Student to Professor to Course. It can be appropriate for class-based queries, such as finding all the Student objects whose last names start with "L." Class-based clustering is like the table-based clustering supported by some relational DBMSs. Table-based clustering is appropriate for many relational databases because of the table orientation of all relational operators. Some relational systems even store all the rows of a table in a separate file dedicated to that table.

MOVING OBJECTS AND RECLAIMING SPACE CAN IMPROVE CLUSTERING

Sometimes an object DBMS needs to be able to move objects on storage to improve clustering. Consider a collection of objects that are stored on a page. Over time the application will delete some of these objects and add new ones. When the object DBMS deletes an object, a hole of unused space is left on the page. The object DBMS can reuse that space to store another object, if that new object fits into the hole. The holes on a page gradually tend to get smaller and smaller, and the probability increases that a new object will not fit on the page. The conventional DBMS techniques for managing storage include consolidation of the holes into a single larger hole, or free space. The object DBMS has to be able to move the objects on the page, which is actually how the holes get moved together and consolidated. Without hole-space consolidation, a collection of requests that once required a single access to disk may over time require multiple page accesses. Sustaining excellent performance over time with considerable delete and insert activity requires fairly intelligent storage-management capability by the object DBMS.

Notice that the expense of consolidating holes may rise significantly if object identifiers are implemented by virtual memory addresses. When the object DBMS moves an object in storage, it cannot invalidate any references to that object. If these references are physical rather than logical, the object DBMS must fix all the references to point correctly to the newly relocated object. This fix-up process typically requires the database to be taken off-line. Logical references, on the other hand, are correct even when the target object moves. The object DBMS can reclaim space on-line.

INDEXING CAN IMPROVE VALUE-BASED ACCESS

Applications can access objects not only by reference, but also by value-based queries. Performance for query access to objects based on their attribute values can be dramatically improved if the object DBMS implements indexes on those attributes. An index may be a simple table of attribute-value address pairs, or it may be a complex branching structure optimized to provide targeted access through large volumes of objects. Over the years the relational DBMS community has developed many indexing techniques, most of which are applicable to object databases as well. Newer techniques have also been developed for indexing objects, which have more complex structural requirements than relational tables, such as nested structures [Bert89] and spatial data [Gutt84].

Access patterns are the main determinant of which attributes should be indexed. If applications only rarely use an attribute in queries, the implementation of that attribute should not be indexed. If a large percentage of the objects in a class extent have the same attribute value (e.g., for the sex attribute), then it probably should not be indexed because the index will not be discriminating. If applications frequently update the values of an attribute, then it perhaps should not be indexed, because the object DBMS will need to update the index as well. There is a clear tradeoff between retrieval performance and update overhead that should be considered in deciding whether to install an index or not.

It is the object DBMS's responsibility to construct and maintain index structures. It is typically an application or database administrator's responsibility to determine which attributes should be indexed. Some object DBMSs may dynamically construct indexes based on detected access patterns, without explicit request from an application or human.

REPLICATION CAN IMPROVE PERFORMANCE IN SINGLE-SITE AND DISTRIBUTED SYSTEMS

Replication is another storage-management technique developers can use to improve performance. Replicated objects are objects for which there is more than one copy. More formally, a replicated object is an object with more than one implementation. The individual elements in the set of implementations of a single object are called *replicas*. The set of replicas of a given object is called its *replication set*. The number of elements in a replication set is referred to as the *degree* of replication of the object. The elements of a replication set are all physical implementations of a single logical object. There may be many different replication sets in a system, each representing a given object and each with a different degree. An object is *completely replicated* if there is at least one element of its replication set stored at every site in the network where the object might be accessed. At the other extreme, a replication set might be minimal and contain only two elements. The appropriate degree of replication is determined by a variety of factors, including object access patterns, relative frequencies of update and retrieval activities, network reliability, processor and media reliability, response time requirements, and so forth.

When an application references a replicated object, the object DBMS has a choice of which replica to access. In general, the application should be completely unaware of which replica is actually being accessed at any given time. The application should not even need to know that an object is replicated, rather than having a single implementation. Management of replicas ideally is a system-level function, not an application function.

The term *replica* is used differently in the context of object databases than in the context of antiques and art. With antiques and art, the distinction is always made between an original and a replica. In object databases, there may or may not be a distinction between the original and other copies. The object DBMS may treat all implementations of an object as peers or may designate one copy as a primary copy.

There is no standard yet for how object databases should handle replicated objects. One issue is how to handle object identity with replication. A reasonable approach is for all replicas of an object to have the same object identifier. This provides the most flexibility for the object database and is consistent with the notion that object identifiers can be used to test the equality of objects. If replicas do not have the same object identifier, then it may be difficult for the object DBMS to determine that they are copies of the same object. It would then become the application's responsibility to manage these replicas.

Not all replicas of an object are necessarily identical. One simple example is when replicas are stored on machines with different architectures. The replica implementations are necessarily different at the lowest level. Another example is when an object is replicated as a C++ object and a Smalltalk object.

REPLICAS MAY BE LOCAL OR DISTRIBUTED

There are many options for how widely to distribute replicas. In some situations, the most appropriate scheme is to store replicas at the same processing site, but on different volumes. This is what would happen if an object DBMS were to use disk mirroring. The object DBMS would store every database object on a primary disk as well as on a secondary disk mirroring the primary. The object DBMS would process every update at both volumes.

In distributed applications it may be more appropriate to store replicas at different processing sites. This approach may be suitable in both local-area and wide-area network environments. Some object DBMSs support hierarchies of databases, enabling users to check out objects from shared group databases on servers into personal databases. When an application checks out an object, the object DBMS creates a replica in the personal database. The replica has the same object identifier as the source object in the group database.

Replicas can also be stored at the same site, even in the same database. For example, consider a financial application that requires access to time-series data about investment prices and returns. The application requires very rapid access to these data sometimes for a particular investment and sometimes for a range of dates. The data might be replicated in the database in two collection structures: one clustering data by security, the other clustering by date. The result would be clustering that satisfies the needs of two kinds of requests with incompatible logical access patterns.

An object's description must be available to the object DBMS wherever that object is replicated. If objects are self-describing, then this replication of the class information is automatic. If objects are described by class objects, then the object DBMS must manage replication of the class information. For instance, when an application checks out objects from a shared group database to a personal database, the object DBMS must also replicate the pertinent class objects in the personal database.

REPLICATION CAN ALSO IMPROVE AVAILABILITY AND SITE AUTONOMY

One objective in replicating objects is to improve performance. Replication for performance can be especially useful in wide-area networks, where transmission times can noticeably affect application response times. In general, avoiding the network means improving application performance. Avoiding the network altogether may imply massive replication if many sites need access to the same objects.

Another objective in replicating objects is to improve availability. If one user or application has reserved exclusive access to an object, then that object is not available to any other users or applications. Maximizing availability at the expense of everything else implies always using replication. Maximum availability occurs when every application that needs access to an object has its own replica. In general, replication improves read performance but introduces additional processing requirements when objects are updated.

A third objective in replicating objects is to improve site autonomy. Site autonomy is achieved if no site is dependent on what happens at other sites. For example, site autonomy is compromised if a failure at one site affects another site. If an object is stored only at one site and if for any reason that object is unavailable due to processor downtime, network interruption, device failure, and so on, any other sites needing access to that object are affected. Their operations are affected by a problem that has occurred at another site. Alternative copies of objects give the system opportunity to respond gracefully to outages. The impacts of failures can be more localized, and applications need not be reliant on single-source objects.

Another, perhaps more subtle, aspect of site autonomy is the positive feeling of ownership and control that comes from having a local replica of important objects. A familiar example is when we make replicas of our tax returns, rather than turning over these objects completely to government agencies. This consideration exists in database situations as well as in paper-based situations.

MANAGING REPLICATED OBJECTS INVOLVES MANY FACTORS

There are many factors that need to be considered in managing replicated objects, including:

- determining the appropriate degree of replication and deciding where replicas should be stored

- synchronizing updates to replicas, so that objects are sufficiently current to meet application needs

- determining which replica to access, so that both performance and currency requirements are met.

Not all objects in a system need the same degree of replication. It may be appropriate for some objects to be completely replicated, while other objects are not replicated at all. Sometimes it is appropriate for applications or users to request explicitly that an object be replicated at runtime. In other situations it is more appropriate for the object DBMS to determine the appropriate degree of replication.

Certain basic tradeoffs apply in managing object replication. In general:

- Increasing replication increases the probability that applications will access local objects, reducing transmission requirements and improving performance.

- Increasing replication increases availability and site autonomy, by reducing sites' dependence on objects stored at other sites.

- Reducing replication reduces the processing required to synchronize updates and improves performance.

- The higher the ratio of update-to-query activity, the greater the processing and transmission required to keep replicas synchronized.

- The greater the number of sources of update activity, the greater the processing and transmission required to keep replicas synchronized.

- Designating one element of a replication set as a master source of updates provides an anchor point for synchronizing updates and simplifies the synchronization process.

- The greater the need for current data, the more frequently that replicas should be synchronized.

The kinds of parameters that should be considered in determining an appropriate object distribution and replication scheme include:

- patterns of access to objects, including access to components of aggregate objects

- relative frequencies of update and query activities

- tolerance for almost-current data versus the need for continual synchronization

- reliability of the environment, with replication providing backup sources

- performance requirements and effects of transmission capacities and speeds.

Because of these tradeoffs and the range of application requirements, no single solution for replication and partitioning management is appropriate for all distributed object systems. A range of mechanisms and policies is required.

For the most part, applications must manage their own object replication and partitioning policies. This is especially true for situations where individual objects have different degrees of replication. The application must determine where replicas should be located, to which replica queries and updates should be routed, and how to synchronize updates. Some object DBMSs provide object compare methods that enable an application to determine whether or not two objects are the same, that is, have the same structure and contents. This functionality is important in cases where application-managed replicas are assigned different object identifiers by the object DBMS, which does not recognize the objects as replicas.

Even when replication management is an application responsibility, there are many situations where it is worthwhile. For example, consider an application deployed in an environment with three LANs, connected by WAN communications. An appropriate design might be to replicate completely an object database in each of the three LANs. Each database would be local to one LAN, and the effects of transmission delays for WAN communication would be minimized. The developers need to determine what to do when a database object is updated in one of the LANs. Complexity can be reduced significantly if one of the three sites is designated to be the master or authority and all updates are processed there. Depending on the volume of updates, that master site either could download complete replacement copies of the database to each of the other two sites or could download batches of the transactions. The developers should determine the frequency of reconciliation based on the extent of update activity and the application's tolerance for use of almost-current replicas. In many situations, however, it is not reasonable to route all updates to a single master site. A more complex synchronization policy is then needed.

For some time now, object DBMSs have included functionality to manage transactions that involve updates to multiple objects, either colocated or stored at different sites in a network. An important aspect of this functionality is two-phase commit, which ensures integrity of transactions that involve multiple sites. Users sometimes expect two-phase commit to have a role in replication management. This is the case only when the application includes updates to replicas in a single transaction. Using two-phase commit and conventional database transactions to control updates to replicas is overkill if the application environment can tolerate delay in synchronization.

Replication of objects can have significant benefits, but it introduces nontrivial object location and synchronization challenges. Object DBMS products are just beginning to offer some features that can help applications manage object replication. Developers must consider application object access patterns and needs for currency in determining the most appropriate policy and techniques to use.

IN CLOSING . . .

Storing and finding persistent objects involves many dimensions, ranging from the process structure and client–server architecture of the object DBMS to the policies and functions provided for handling replicated objects. Because the object DBMS products use various techniques for implementing object identifiers, for working with programming language constructs like pointers, for implementing relationship traversal paths, for clustering objects, and for speeding access through indexes, there can be considerable difference in the performance that object DBMS products can deliver on a particular application.

CHAPTER 8

Object Sharing

A fundamental characteristic of an object database is that it can support object sharing. Many applications require this functionality. In practically all situations where multiple users need to access the same data, controls are required to prevent the users from interfering with each other. There are many sources of interference; several are introduced in this chapter. The fundamental principle is that a user should be able to complete a logical unit of work, known in database terminology as a *transaction*, without another user being able to alter the actions of the first. The features an object DBMS provides to prevent multiuser interference are generally referred to as "concurrency control" and "transaction management" functionality. These techniques are also important in supporting database recovery.

Some of the techniques provided by the object DBMSs are the same as those provided by the relational DBMS products. This chapter will first introduce these traditional database sharing techniques, and then will turn to the additional techniques that the object DBMSs offer to address other requirements. The traditional techniques have been perfected over the years to support on-line transaction processing (OLTP), which comprises highly focused, short-duration database activities, such as debiting or crediting an individual's bank account. The additional requirements addressed by the object DBMSs are raised by activities of longer duration, such as modifying the design of a part or analyzing the performance of a financial portfolio under particular economic conditions. Client–server and distributed computing applications cause additional modification of the traditional sharing-control mechanisms.

CONCURRENCY CONTROL PREVENTS INTERFERENCE

Whenever two or more users or programs attempt to share objects, there is the potential for their actions to interfere with each other. The purpose of concurrency control is to maintain a desirable level of database consistency, regardless of how many users or programs are accessing the same objects and even if there are system crashes. "Consistency" here is used as a more-or-less formal word, with particular connotations. Let's first understand what consistency is and the kinds of situations that can threaten it.

Determining whether or not a collection of objects is consistent means determining if the collection adheres to a set of application-defined rules. These rules can be very simple. For example, "A always equals B." Keeping a collection consistent at all times is impossible if there are updates or changes to the objects. Consider a program that adds 2 to the implementation of an attribute of both A and B, which we'll call `a` and `b`, respectively. At some point A's attribute will have been updated and B's will not, or vice versa. The two actions cannot take place simultaneously, except with the support of multiple synchronized processors. If the initial state is `a=b=10`, then at the point where `a=12` and `b=10`, the consistency rule "A always equals B" is violated.

The database cannot always meet consistency rules after individual actions. Instead, an application typically expects that *sets* of actions will preserve consistency. Each set of actions carries objects from a consistent state to a possibly inconsistent temporary state, and then again to a consistent state. Such a set of actions is considered to be an atomic, logical unit of work and is called a "transaction." Transaction management is the task of ensuring that transactions preserve consistency.

Object DBMSs generally require that applications do all access, creation, modification, and deletion of persistent objects within transactions. Database operations must execute within the bounds of transaction controls. Object DBMSs therefore provide functions for the programmer to use to specify transaction beginning and ending points. An ending point—either a commit or an abort—is a synchronization point. The object DBMS ensures at the synchronization point that the objects are in a consistent state, either by guaranteeing that all updates made by the user since the end of the last transaction are successfully done or by guaranteeing that none of those updates is done.

SIDEBAR: TRANSACTION PROPERTIES

A database transaction has three basic properties:

1. It is application-defined. This means that it obeys the application's rules of consistency. The DBMS cannot determine what is and what is not logically a transaction. This is the application's responsibility.

2. It is all or nothing. The transaction happens either in its entirety or not at all. Either all of its updates take effect and the transaction is said to *commit*, or none of the updates survives and the transaction is said to *abort*. A transaction cannot be left partially complete.

3. It cannot be undone. Once a transaction commits, its updates cannot be backed out. Its results can be altered only by the actions of subsequent transactions.

A transaction therefore has only two possible outcomes: committed or aborted. A committed transaction has reached a successful end; an aborted transaction has encountered some difficulty and has an unsuccessful ending. An aborted transaction cannot be allowed to leave any of its updates in the database. All of a transaction's actions must be completed, or none of them. For example, a transaction that is intended to update 25 account objects cannot end with only 12 of them changed. A transaction that is intended to translate a solid figure in x, y, z space and then rotate it by 180 degrees cannot end with the translation actions done but the rotation actions incomplete. If a transaction aborts, the object DBMS must take appropriate action to ensure that the results of none of that transaction's actions are persistent.

The application must specify a transaction's boundaries. A transaction is a logical unit of work, and only the application logic can determine whether it is mandatory that all 25 accounts be updated together. If the updates could stand separately, then the application would more appropriately specify each account's update as a separate transaction, rather than bundling all 25 updates into a single transaction. Only the application can determine whether it is mandatory that the translation and rotation of the solid mentioned above happen together. If the application really has other motion dependencies, then the programmer should include those dependent actions in the transaction.

Sometimes the situation that necessitates a transaction abort is induced by the "system." For example, there could be a media failure, a power outage, or a conflict detected between users. Other times it is the user's decision to abort a transaction. For example, after making some exploratory updates to a product design object, the engineer might decide that the design changes are not working out as expected and that the updates should not be saved.

Concurrent access is relatively easy for an object database to support if no users are changing object states. But whenever multiple programs or users are accessing a collection of objects concurrently and at least one of them is updating the state of one or more objects, there can be interference, which can result in inconsistency. Three kinds of inconsistencies that can be avoided through appropriate concurrency control techniques are lost updates, assumed updates, and inconsistent reads. These are all situations where a transaction that is correct when run in isolation produces incorrect results when run with another transaction. The interference is caused by the interleaving of the actions of the two transactions. Concurrency control is largely intended to avoid the interleaving situations that cause consistency problems. These consistency problems are well known in relational database management.

Consider the situation illustrated in Fig. 8-1. User 1 intends to add 2 to the value of x, which is a state variable of some object. User 2 intends to multiply the value of x for that object by 2. Users 1 and 2 start their actions

FIGURE 8-1.
INTERFERENCE RESULTING IN LOST UPDATE.

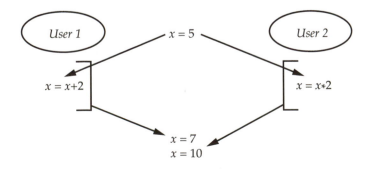

at nearly the same time. Both read the value of x as 10. User 1 updates the value of x to 12, while user 2 updates the value of x to 20. Whichever user finishes last will determine what value x has: either 12 or 20. The effect of one or the other's update is lost. Neither of them even considers the results of the other's actions. If the transactions had not been interleaved, x would have been left either with the value 24 (add 2 to 10, then multiply by 2), or with the value 22 (multiply by 2, then add 2). Either sequential execution of user 1 and 2's updates prevents interference and the loss of one of their updates.

Consider another interference situation, illustrated in Fig. 8-2. This example uses the same intended actions as above. Users 1 and 2 execute their actions serially rather than being interleaved, but user 1's actions abort due to some failure. User 2 accesses the object and uses 1's results before the abort occurs. The effect is that user 2 assumes that user 1's actions complete successfully, even though that update is subsequently undone.

Another interference situation is illustrated in Fig. 8-3. Here user 1 is sequencing through an ordered collection of objects, summing their values for a particular state variable x. Meanwhile, user 2 updates a couple of the

FIGURE 8-2.
INTERFERENCE RESULTING IN ASSUMED UPDATE.

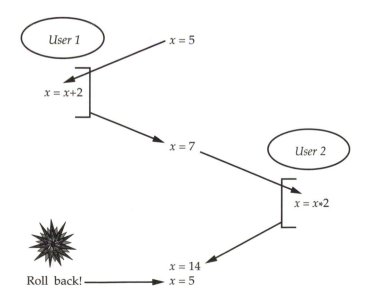

FIGURE 8-3.

INTERFERENCE RESULTING IN INCONSISTENT READ.

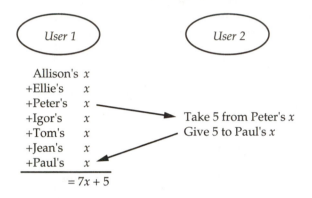

Allison's x
+Ellie's x
+Peter's x
+Igor's x Take 5 from Peter's x
+Tom's x Give 5 to Paul's x
+Jean's x
+Paul's x
———————————
            $= 7x + 5$

objects, transferring 5 from x in the Peter object into the value of x in the Paul object. Because user 1 adds Peter's contribution before the 5 is transferred out and then adds Paul's contribution after the 5 is transferred in, user 1's result is 5 greater than it would have been if user 2's move-from-Peter-to-Paul transaction had not been executing concurrently. User 2's work has interfered with user 1's.

In each of these cases, the updates of one user have interfered with either the reads or the updates of another. It is the object DBMS's responsibility to ensure that these kinds of interference do not occur. There is a formal criterion from relational database theory for assessing whether a set of actions has been executed in a consistent way:

> A database is said to be *consistent* if its state after execution of a set of transactions is exactly the same as if those transactions had executed serially.

This definition comes directly from conventional database technology and is used by the relational DBMS vendors as well as the object DBMS vendors. The definition does not require that the transactions actually execute serially; it only requires that the results be the same as if they had executed serially. For example, in Fig. 8-1, either 24 or 22 is considered to be a consistent answer. 24 is obtained if user 1's actions execute first, then user 2's; 22 is obtained if user 2's actions execute first, then user 1's. In the assumed update example, user 1's aborted actions may occur either before or after user 2's actions, with a consistent result. The inconsistency is a result of user 2's actions being dependent on subsequently aborted actions. In the inconsistent read example, user 1 may collect its total value for x either before or after user 2 updates objects in the collection, with a consistent result. The inconsistent read results from the interaction between users 1's and 2's activities.

This definition of consistency is sometimes unsettling. How can there be more than one consistent result to execution of a set of transactions? How can either 24 or 22 be a consistent answer? The object DBMS cannot determine which is the correct sequence. If it matters whether user 1's actions occur before user 2's, then their actions should be explicitly serialized. For example, if user 1 is giving all employees a 3 percent cost-of-living wage increase and user 2 is selectively adding individualized merit increases, then there is probably a business policy that dictates which action should take place first. This determination is part of the application logic and is not the object DBMS's responsibility.

SIDEBAR: SERIALIZABLE EXECUTION

When a DBMS executes transactions serially, all the actions of one are processed and then all the actions of the next are processed. There is no concurrency. This is called *serial execution*. When executed serially, transactions cannot interfere with each other; only one is active at a time. This is one approach to guaranteeing consistency, but it typically is not practical in multiuser systems. Instead the actions of multiple users are interleaved under DBMS control, with the objective of increasing the level of concurrency in the system—satisfying more users in a given period, while maintaining consistency.

Interleaving transactions does not always result in inconsistency. An interleaved execution of transactions is said to be *serializable* if it produces the same result as some serial (i.e., noninterleaved) execution of those same transactions. Achieving serializability is sometimes called *transaction isolation*. If an object DBMS generates only serializable executions of transactions, then it is said to guarantee consistency. Serializable concurrent transactions accessing shared objects cannot interfere with each other.

Consider Mike and Sam, both of whom are working with the design of a particular mechanical part. Mike's transaction calculates the weight of the part, and Sam's transaction replicates a pair of holes in that same part, leaving the part with four holes. There are two serializable executions of these two transactions, each giving a different, but consistent result. An inconsistent execution would calculate the weight of the part after only some of the hole replication process had completed. If the order of execution of Mike's and Sam's transactions is significant, then they should be combined into one transaction: either "calculate the weight, then replicate the pair of holes," or "replicate the pair of holes, then calculate the weight." If the transactions are somehow interdependent, then they should not be isolated, but should instead be bounded by the application as a single transaction.

OBJECT DBMSs USE LOCKS TO PREVENT INTERFERENCE

The most common approach object DBMSs use to guarantee serializable executions is a technique called *locking*, borrowed from relational DBMSs. In its simplest form, locking an object prevents other transactions from using that object until the lock has been released. It is the object DBMS's responsibility to manage locks. Managing locks includes granting locks to transactions on particular objects in response to their lock requests, keeping track of which transactions hold which locks, detecting when lock requests would interfere with each other, and clearing locks when transactions have released them. It is sometimes the application's responsibility to specify which objects should be locked.

SIDEBAR: LOCKING

Both object and relational DBMSs offer several kinds of locks. The two most fundamental kinds are *exclusive locks* and *shared locks*. Only one transaction may hold an exclusive lock on a particular object. That lock prevents all other transactions from accessing the object in any way. By contrast, multiple transactions may concurrently hold shared locks on a particular object. The shared lock allows these transactions to access the object concurrently. However, holding a shared lock does not permit the transaction to update the object. A transaction must acquire an exclusive lock on an object to be able to update that object. Exclusive locks are therefore often called *write locks*, and shared locks are often called *read locks*. Multiple requests for read locks on an object do not conflict with each other and can all be granted concurrently by the DBMS. Multiple requests for write locks on an object do conflict with each other and only one can be granted by the DBMS at any given time.

To help increase concurrency when there are programs that do not need guaranteed consistency, some DBMSs support *dirty reads*. When a transaction accesses an object in dirty read mode, it basically is requesting that the locking mechanism be bypassed altogether for that object. A dirty read ignores any locks that other transactions may hold and proceeds to access the object regardless of whether some other transaction may be updating it. For example, an application might access a collection of project objects to scan their objectives and status, without caring whether another application might be updating one of those objects. An application might access a large collection of employee objects to calculate an average salary, without regard for whether another application might be updating a few of those employees' salaries during the scan. Using dirty reads where appropriate is an important way to increase system concurrency. It is the characteristics of applications that determine whether or not dirty reads are appropriate. The object DBMS cannot decide this.

There are a variety of ways that DBMSs physically lock objects. Some DBMSs keep tables recording the identifiers of locked objects; others set bits in locked objects. Another technique is to move all locked objects to a specified area of memory. Locking mechanisms can have considerable influence on database overhead requirements and performance.

It typically is appropriate for a transaction to hold locks on many objects. These are the objects accessed during the transaction. Some of these locks can be exclusive and some can be shared. To simplify the programmer's job, some object DBMSs automatically request locks when the application references objects. In these situations, the locking mechanism is invisible to the programmer. In other situations, it is more appropriate for the application explicitly to request particular kinds of locks. In general, an object DBMS implicitly grants shared locks to referenced objects, unless the application explicitly requests exclusive locks or requests that an object not be locked at all.

When an application needs to request locks explicitly, it is convenient for the programmer to be able to request locks on an entire collection of objects rather than to request a lock individually on each member of the collection. The basic tradeoff in determining how much of a database to lock is that while it may be convenient to lock a large collection (maybe even an entire database) of objects all at once, those locks limit other transactions' access.

JUDICIOUS LOCKING CAN INCREASE CONCURRENCY

In general, the more objects that a particular transaction locks, the lower the level of concurrency that the object database can support during that transaction. Any objects locked in exclusive mode are not available for other transactions to read or write. Any objects locked in shared mode are not available for other transactions to write. Thus, locking only needed objects is one way to increase concurrency. When a transaction is waiting for locked objects to become available, the object database is not supporting as high a degree of concurrency as it would if that transaction were executing.

Another way to increase concurrency is to request the weakest form of lock that meets the transaction's needs. If the transaction is going to update an object, then it needs an exclusive lock on that object. On the other hand, if the transaction is not going to update an object, then it does not need to request an exclusive lock. In general, requesting the same kind of lock for all objects referenced by a transaction will result in overlimiting concurrency. Requesting the particular kind of lock suited for a transaction's actions on particular objects will increase concurrency.

Sometimes two or more transactions are blocked waiting for locks held by each other to be released. Neither can continue processing until it acquires a lock held by the other, and neither intends to release any locks it holds. This situation is called *deadlock*. There are ways for an object DBMS to prevent this kind of situation from occurring. One technique is for the object DBMS to require that a transaction request and acquire all the locks it will need in one indivisible operation at the beginning of the transaction. This technique is generally unrealistic for situations where transactions do not necessarily know which objects they will access at runtime. If the technique is used, then transactions generally lock entire databases. This large-scale locking enables the transaction to meet both the object DBMS's requirements and its own application's requirements, but it can significantly limit the number of users that the object database can support concurrently.

A less limiting technique is for the object DBMS to maintain graphs that record which transactions are waiting for which locks and which transactions hold which locks. If the object DBMS never grants locks that would cause "wait-for" cycles to appear in these graphs, then deadlock will not occur. This technique, however, is somewhat difficult to implement, especially in distributed environments, where a transaction at one site may need objects at another site in order to proceed. The object DBMS at each site would maintain its own wait-for graph, and these multiple object DBMSs would need to be able to share their graphs in order to detect cycles across them (see Fig. 8-4).

Because of the difficulty of detecting intersite deadlock using wait-for graphs, object DBMSs that support distributed transactions typically use a combination of detecting cycles in local wait-for graphs and a time-out mechanism for intersite waits. The object DBMS detects deadlock situations by tracking the amount of time that processes spend in a suspended state waiting for locks to be acquired. There is a system-configurable "time-out" limit set to control the length of waiting time. When a process is suspended past this limit, the object DBMS generally aborts that process's active transaction, releases its locks, and the deadlock situation is resolved. In some cases, deadlock will remain, but eventually another process will time out, its transaction will be aborted, its locks released, and so forth.

FIGURE 8-4.
WAIT-FOR GRAPHS SPANNING SITES.

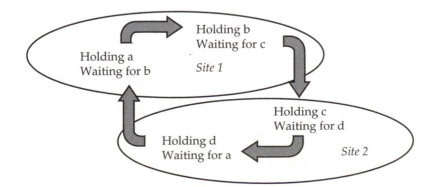

A user or application rarely notices when deadlock occurs, because in most database environments locks are typically held only for short periods, since transactions are of very short duration. The time-out limit is commonly set at a second or less. Longer duration transactions require different concurrency control techniques, which we'll discuss later.

OBJECT DBMSs USE LOGS TO COMMIT OR ABORT TRANSACTIONS

A common reason for a transaction to abort is system failure. Nearly all computer systems fail at times. Being able to recover from these failures is a DBMS responsibility. Applications and users should not have to figure out how to bring databases out of the failure situation. By contrast, if a laptop computer should freeze during a text editing session, the user typically has only one recourse: restart the machine and revert to the state of the file as of the last time it was saved. It is the user's responsibility to determine when to save files and onto what media to save them.

In a shared database environment, however, the database does not belong to an individual, but rather it is accessed and used by many users and applications. The object DBMS takes on the responsibilities of automatically making backup copies and of recovering databases when there are failures. Somewhat different techniques are used depending on the scope of the failure. If a single transaction aborts, then the object DBMS has to recover only that transaction. If there is a system failure, then the object DBMS has to recover all running transactions.

Aborting a transaction simply means that its updates cannot be written to the database persistent storage. Either the updates have been made only in main memory and do not need to be written to the log or database, or some updates may have already been written to the log or database. These latter updates must be backed out by the object DBMS, usually by applying before-images from the log (see the sidebar on logging).

SIDEBAR: LOGGING

An object or relational DBMS typically uses a technique called *logging* to both abort and commit transactions. A log is simply making an auxiliary record of object state for use by the DBMS. The log exists in addition to the persistent record that applications use. The log is used only by the DBMS and is not visible to applications. It is essential to nearly all transaction management and recovery capabilities. A log is like an auxiliary database that is used by the DBMS to ensure recoverability of update actions.

The records that a DBMS writes to a log are typically of two types:

- A *before-image* is a copy of an object's state before a transaction's updates have been applied.

- An *after-image* is a copy of an object's state after a transaction's updates have been applied.

Before-images are used by the DBMS to undo any updates that may have been written to persistent storage by transactions that must be aborted. The DBMS simply replaces the object's updated state with the state recorded in the before-image. After-images are used by the DBMS to apply updates by transactions that need to commit but have been interrupted by some failure during the commit process (Fig. 8-5). Log records typically include an identifier for the associated program or user, a time-stamp, and other pertinent information.

FIGURE 8-5.
APPLICATION OF BEFORE- AND AFTER-IMAGES.

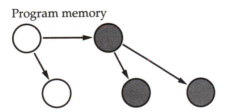

Before-Image   After-Image   Database

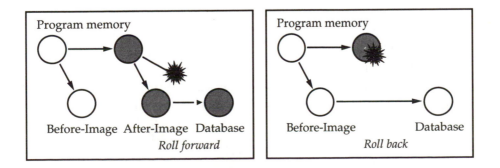

Many DBMSs use a technique called *write-ahead logging* to ensure that persistent log records are available for transaction recovery. This technique simply is a protocol that requires the DBMS always to write its image records to the log before writing the corresponding state updates to persistent storage.

One way to understand the need for write-ahead logging is to consider what can happen if it were not used. Suppose that the database were updated first, then the log records were written. If a failure were to occur, say the network went down in a client–server environment, after the database had been changed but before the log records were written, there would be no log records to use if transaction recovery were necessary. Changes would have been made to the database without information about those changes being written to the log. The DBMS would have lost its capability to remove the database updates should the transaction abort. With write-ahead logging, the DBMS always has recorded in the log the information needed to recover a transaction, before the transaction's updates are made in the database.

Recovering all running transactions is more complicated. Each will be in one of several possible situations. Some transactions will not yet have reached their commit or abort points. None of the updates of these work-in-process transactions can stay in the database. The object DBMS typically handles them as if it were aborting individual transactions, applying before-images from the log. Any changed objects are returned to their states prior to the start of the interrupted transactions.

Some other transactions may be in the process of aborting when the system failure occurs. The object DBMS must ensure that these aborts complete. The object DBMS uses the before-images for the aborting transactions, applying them to the affected objects and completing the abort by rolling back changes that may have been in progress.

Other transactions may be in the process of committing when the failure occurs. The object DBMS must ensure that these commits complete, because it guarantees that all of these transactions' updates will be written to the database persistent storage. Some may already have been written; others may still reside in main memory caches. During the commit process the object DBMS flushes the cache to persistent storage. If the commit process is interrupted by a failure, then the object DBMS can use logged after-images rather than the cache as the source of updates. Applying an after-image is like redoing an update.

The caveat here is that the object DBMS must have logged after-images as the application progressed in order to have them available to complete the commits. If performance considerations require choosing between before- and after-imaging, but not using both, then it is typical to select before-imaging. The object DBMS can then roll back any incomplete transactions to their beginnings, even if their commit process is underway when the failure occurs.

The performance of an object database is affected by many factors, an important one of which is the overhead introduced by logging and transaction management. Logging after-images basically doubles the number of writes to persistent storage: one write for the log record and one for the database. Some object DBMSs offer options to help minimize logging overhead. For example, if only a small part of a very large object is being updated, then that part of the object affected by the update could be logged, rather than making the auxiliary copy of the entire object. Conversely, if many smaller objects are being updated together, then they could be logged together with fewer writes from the cache than if they were logged separately.

Some object DBMSs offer the user or database administrator options to selectively turn on or off logging of before- or after-images. Turning off logging can significantly improve performance, but it leaves databases open to the liability of not being able to recover completely from failures. Sometimes performance benchmarks are run with logging turned off to maximize the throughput and minimize the response time numbers. In some situations it can be quite appropriate to turn off the recovery mechanism, for example, during prototyping.

SIDEBAR: DATABASE BACKUPS

Just like many users periodically create backup copies of their personal files, an object DBMS can also make backup copies of databases. Some object DBMSs provide functions that enable a database administrator to specify the interval for making backups. The volume of updates, value of database contents, and expected failure rate of the system are all parameters that should be considered in determining the backup interval.

Many production environments require that the object DBMS be able to make on-line backups, rather than making databases unavailable to applications and users while backup copies are made. On-line backup processing may perceptively slow performance. However, this slowdown is generally considered to be a reasonable tradeoff for the higher availability and recoverability offered when the object DBMS makes on-line backups at appropriate intervals. Otherwise, a database administrator typically schedules periodic downtime for purposes of making backup copies and doing other administrative tasks.

OBJECT DBMSs SUPPORT DISTRIBUTED TRANSACTIONS

Supporting transactions with distributed databases introduces additional complications for the object DBMS. One of these was introduced here in conjunction with detecting deadlock situations caused by transactions on different sites waiting for locks that each other already hold. Another challenge for the object DBMS is ensuring commitment for transactions that update objects resident at multiple sites. The object DBMS must be able to guarantee transaction integrity in situations more complex than the single-site case. The network connections between sites may go down, and processors involved in the transaction may fail.

The most widely publicized approach to coordinating distributed transactions is the two-phase commit protocol (see the next sidebar). The architecture of many of the object DBMS products enables the transaction coordinator to reside in the client part of the object DBMS. This is in contrast to the relational database architecture, where only a thin layer of DBMS functionality resides on the client side. The relational architecture places the transaction coordinator function on the server side. Either one relational database server takes on the role of master and coordinates the other servers, or any server can act as coordinator. The master–server situation can reduce site autonomy and introduce unacceptable dependence on one site. The other approach introduces difficulties of peer-to-peer coordination. Adding either master-site or peer-to-peer transaction coordination to an inherently centralized relational DBMS has been a difficult design and implementation task for some DBMS vendors. The object DBMSs were initially designed for distributed systems, and they benefit from client-side transaction coordination, which has been somewhat easier to implement.

It is important to understand that the application itself should not get involved in the two-phase commit procedure; the coordination is the responsibility of the object DBMS and should occur automatically. Because the protocol introduces a significant amount of overhead, it is highly desirable for the object DBMS to invoke the protocol only for truly distributed transactions that update objects at multiple sites. If a transaction accesses objects at only one site or accesses objects at multiple sites but only updates objects at one, then the two-phase commit procedure can be bypassed as unnecessary.

This low-level support can address the needs of some high availability systems that require 24-hour per day, 7-day per week database accessibility, with planned downtime measured in minutes per year. Chapter 7 introduced replication as a technique for increasing availability. Replicated copies can be updated in a single transaction with two-phase commit used to ensure that distributed copies are consistently handled. This approach may be appropriate if it is acceptable for the application to manage replicas, explicitly updating each.

A more appropriate action might be for the DBMS to maintain duplicate databases, also known as *mirrored databases*. Updates are mirrored and directed at both copies, while reads are directed to just one of the copies, which is known as the primary copy. Because the other copy is kept updated, it is known as a *hot standby*. It is always ready to take over. If the primary copy should fail or become inaccessible for any reason, then the DBMS redirects reads to the hot standby and processing continues uninterrupted. Before the failed copy comes back on line, any interim updates are applied to synchronize it with the active database.

The mirrored databases typically reside on different devices to ensure that media, channel, or processor failure does not make both copies unusable at the same time. Some systems might even be implemented with more than two mirrored copies, depending on the probability of failure and the need for availability. A DBMS that supports mirrored databases would typically work with disk mirroring support from the operating system, rather than imposing two-phase commit over the disks.

SIDEBAR: TWO-PHASE COMMIT PROTOCOL

The two-phase commit protocol dictates a sequence of steps that enable the DBMS to determine either that all the actions of the transaction can be committed at all sites participating in the transaction, or that none of the actions will be recorded persistently. Pertinent terminology includes the following:

- The transaction as a whole is called the *distributed transaction*.
- The part of the distributed transaction that is to execute at a particular site is called that site's *local subtransaction*.
- The part of the DBMS that coordinates the distributed transaction is called the *transaction coordinator*.
- The part of the DBMS that is resident at a particular site and manages its local subtransactions is called a *local transaction manager*.

When the application requests that a distributed transaction commit, the transaction coordinator does the following:

Phase 1: Checking Readiness to Commit.

- The transaction coordinator sends a message to each participating local transaction manager asking if it is ready to commit its local subtransaction.
- Each local transaction manager checks whether it is ready to commit the local subtransaction and replies accordingly to the transaction coordinator. Being ready to commit means that the updates of the local subtransaction have been successfully written to the log. The local transaction manager can ensure that no matter what happens next, it has recorded sufficient information to enable the local part of the transaction to commit. The local transaction manager then waits for further instruction from the transaction coordinator.

Phase 2: Go Ahead to Commit or Abort.

• The transaction coordinator collects replies.

• If all the participating local transaction managers indicate that they are ready to commit, then the transaction coordinator sends a message to each telling it to go ahead and commit, writing its updates to persistent storage. However, if any of the participating local transaction managers either does not reply or indicates that it cannot commit, then the transaction coordinator sends a message to all the local transaction managers telling them to abort the transaction.

• The local transaction managers either commit or abort according to the transaction coordinator's instructions.

A variety of difficulties in design and performance can arise in implementing the two-phase commit protocol. The design must accommodate failures at any point in the process. Performance can be severely impacted when failures occur. For example, if the transaction coordinator should fail while the local transaction managers are waiting for their phase 2 instructions, they must continue to wait until the coordinator is back up. If the link to a local transaction manager should fail during phase 2 before it receives its instructions from the coordinator, the coordinator must be prepared to wait until the link is again available to retransmit the instructions.

SOMETIMES TWO-PHASE COMMIT IS TOO HEAVY

There are other situations where two-phase commit introduces too much overhead to be of value. For example, consider an inventory database with a distributed retail application that tracks sales. Assume that sales results are recorded locally in a retail outlet and in an aggregate database at a regional warehouse location. It is highly unlikely that keeping the local retail database and the regional warehouse database synchronized to reflect the sale of individual pencils will be cost-effective. The cost of the two-phase commit process is probably somewhat greater than the profit margin on the sale of a pencil.

Business tradeoffs here indicate that processing updates locally and downloading them in batch to update the regional database is a more reasonable approach. This is just one example where asynchronous updates are suitable. The value of the individual update is considerably less than the value of synchronization. Another way to look at this situation is from a business decision-making perspective. The value of the pencil-purchase update is extremely low because no decisions will be made based on the update. The value of a batch of pencil-purchase updates is higher, because a restocking decision or distributor-contact decision might be made based on the aggregate update. This kind of situation suggests that application developers should be able to specify when it is appropriate for the object DBMS to invoke two-phase commit, and when another technique would suffice.

SOME APPLICATIONS TOLERATE OUT-OF-SYNCH UPDATES

Consider another situation in the banking industry, with credit-card account objects stored at site 1 and checking account objects stored at site 2. Sites 1 and 2 are connected by a wide-area network spanning several hundred miles. When a customer requests a cash advance from his credit-card account to be deposited in his checking account, he would certainly prefer that the bank treat his actions as a single transaction. From a customer perspective, it is unsatisfactory for the cash advance to be recorded, but for the credit to the checking account to fail. However, there are satisfactory alternatives to two-phase commit for managing the updates, even for OLTP applications.

Consider a three-phase process that deals with the credit-card and checking account updates as separate transactions, and introduces a third transaction to manage the synchronization while not affecting response times. The process is as follows.

1. *Transaction 1, executed at site 1:*

   Debit the credit-card account object.

   Write a record of the debit to a log at site 1.

2. *Transaction 2, executed at site 2:*

   Credit the checking account object.

3. *Transaction 3, executed at site 1:*

   Delete the log record of the debit.

Rather than guaranteeing synchronization, the approach here is for the application to tolerate lack of synchronization, while bounding the scope of in-doubt activity such that people can resolve problems it may introduce. If transaction 1 fails, then neither transaction 2 nor 3 is started. If transaction 2 fails, then transaction 3 is not started and a debit record will be in the log for reconciliation by bank personnel as an exception. If transaction 3 fails, the accounts will already be synchronized, and bank personnel will handle the debit record in the log as an entry that requires no further action. From the bank's perspective there is not even any urgency in resolving the exceptions. The appropriateness of this approach is based on the basic business tradeoff that it is of greater value to be able to handle more concurrent users without the time delays incurred by two-phase commit than it is to keep these two account records absolutely synchronized using two-phase commit.

This is an example of a situation that is not handled well either by using two-phase commit (because it is too expensive) or by avoiding two-phase commit. Avoiding the protocol makes it the application's responsibility to code its logic as three separate transactions and to manage the log, which exists solely for purposes of update reconciliation.

SOME TRANSACTIONS LAST A LONG TIME

Another example of a situation where additional application control may be needed and conventional relational database transaction management techniques may not be appropriate is a transaction to process a business travel request. The transaction involves multiple steps: submitting the request; getting appropriate levels of approval; obtaining airline, car, and hotel reservations; generating cash advances; and so forth. Such a procedure is likely to execute for several days. If at any time the trip is cancelled, then updates made so far need to be undone. The user aborts the transaction, so the updates cannot commit. Workflow applications automate this kind of transaction and need recovery mechanisms that relational database transaction management techniques do not provide.

The relational database techniques assume that a transaction is very short and accesses a small amount of data. If a transaction requests a lock on an object that is already locked by another transaction, it may have to wait. If the wait is longer than a short, prespecified period, usually a few seconds, the requesting transaction is typically aborted automatically by the DBMS and the transaction's work is rolled back. Since the lifetime of a conventional transaction is significantly shorter than that of the containing application, it is acceptable for one application to wait for another's locks to be released.

Broadening the perspective of transaction management past conventional OLTP applications leads to recognition that many applications have long-lasting logical units of work. For example, software development, computer-aided design, computer-aided publishing, financial and economic analysis, urban planning, and other areas have logical units of work that may last for days or longer. Conventional locking techniques simply are not applicable, because the resultant level of concurrency would be unacceptable. One engineer working on a product design cannot lock all other engineers out of efforts to access that design for weeks at a time. And weeks of work cannot be simply rolled back because of some problem that occurs near the end of the transaction.

Other complications arise in transactions that involve the execution of multiple processes. For example, consider a transaction in which a software developer wants to edit a source-code file, compile the changed code, and run a particular test. If any of these steps fail, the developer wants the source code to revert to its state prior to the edit step. If all the steps end normally, the developer wants the source code to retain its changed state. Each of the edit, compile, and test steps executes in a separate process, yet all logically belong in a single, long transaction.

Some object DBMSs support long transactions in response to the requirements of these kinds of applications. Long transactions differ from short transactions in several ways:

- Duration. A long transaction can stay open as long as the application requires, while a short transaction will be aborted by the object DBMS if its lock requests are not serviceable.

- Decision to abort. This becomes the application's responsibility in a long transaction, while it is typically made by the object DBMS for a short transaction due to failure of the system or a link or the unavailability of locks.

• Proceed options. Since long transactions can be open for indefinite periods, the application must be able to specify what to do if it cannot acquire objects it needs or if it encounters a failure situation. Options might include waiting for objects, queueing its requests, abandoning its requests, and continuing down an alternate logical path.

The object DBMS needs to provide different techniques to support applications characterized by long transactions [Daya91], [Garc91], [Gray81], [Kort88], [Kung81]. These applications need concurrent access to object databases, with assurance that their update activities will not compromise the integrity or consistency of the objects. Conventional locking techniques do not suffice. Long transactions need to be durable and outlast one or more system failures. An application may check out objects from a database server and retain those objects for several days, perhaps without even being connected to the network. Even if the server site should fail, the object DBMS must retain knowledge of which applications have which objects checked out and with what kinds of locks. Locks therefore must be persistently stored.

COEXISTING VERSIONS CAN ENABLE CONCURRENCY CONTROL

One approach to managing long transactions is called *multiversion concurrency control*. This technique allows multiple transactions to work with their own coexisting versions of shared objects. Multiversion concurrency control supports multiple users' access to (typically compound) objects, while minimizing conflicts through careful analysis of the sequence of users' interleaved reads and writes. The technique requires the object DBMS to dynamically reorder user actions to avoid conflicts. If unavoidable conflicts do occur, then the object DBMS notifies users and interactively negotiates reconciliation.

Rather than attempting to impose solutions to conflicts automatically, the object DBMS leaves resolution to applications or people. For example, consider a situation where two engineers are using a CAD system to design a part. One engineer might be changing a feature on the top surface, while the other is attaching legs to the bottom surface. Since these engineers' actions never actually update the same regions of the part, no conflict occurs. However, if the first user were changing a feature on the bottom surface, then the object DBMS could detect the accesses to the shared surface, issue a notification to the engineers, and expect them to decide which action should go first. Some conflicts may be difficult to detect. For example, yet another engineer might be changing the material that the part is to be composed of, with the result that the part can no longer handle the stress imposed by the added feature.

Most object DBMSs do not yet actively minimize conflicts by dynamically analyzing activity. However, several of the products allow multiple versions of an object to coexist. Different users can concurrently access the versions without interference. The object DBMS does not reconcile differences between the coexisting versions, but may provide difference and merge functions to assist reconciliation.

For example, a widget design department might have several engineers working on variants of the design of a particular part. In a paper-based engineering environment, there is typically a library of design documents and a protocol for checking out documents, modifying designs, approving them, and checking the revised documents back into the library for shared access. Engineering organizations typically develop precise numbering schemes to track the evolution of designs through multiple versions.

Some organizations allow several engineers to check out a design document concurrently. Each checked-in modification then becomes a new version of the design. The version history can be represented as a *version derivation graph*, showing the precedence relationships between the versions (see Fig. 8-6). The graph can branch either when multiple engineers derive different versions concurrently from the same design document, or when

FIGURE 8-6.
VERSION DERIVATION HISTORY GRAPH WITH VERSION BRANCHING.

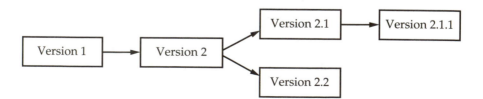

an engineer goes back to a noncurrent version and starts a new derivation from the older version. Sometimes a version derivation history graph shows a merge of two versions into a single version, with further derivations proceeding from there (see Fig. 8-7).

This paper-based model of check-out and check-in, with careful maintenance of version derivation history information, is also the basis of multiversion concurrency control for databases. Some object DBMSs provide functions for checking objects in and out of shared databases into private workspaces. Some also provide functions for tracking versioning histories, such as `find_predecessors`, `find_successors`. Object DBMSs do not, however, provide logic for determining when a version derivation graph should branch or for determining how to merge versions. Applications must supply this logic.

Supporting versions allows multiple users to share access to the same objects, enabling each to update those objects as necessary without interfering with other users. The definition of consistency is left to the application, which is responsible for reconciliation of different users' versions of an object. This approach matches closely the concurrency control mechanisms developed over the years for group design environments. The value of enabling concurrent access is greater than the effort required to keep all versions exactly the same. In fact, in some applications it would be undesirable to keep all versions identical.

VERSIONING AND LONG TRANSACTIONS REQUIRE NEW MECHANISMS

Versioning and long transactions are not inextricably tied to object DBMSs; they could be offered by relational DBMS products as well.

FIGURE 8-7.
VERSION DERIVATION HISTORY GRAPH WITH VERSION MERGING.

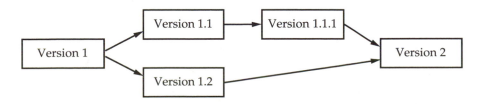

However, new mechanisms are required to manage both versioning and long transactions. Some mechanisms require programmer interfaces; others should be invoked automatically by the DBMS. For example, consider a document object. If one component chapter is revised, that update could be reflected either as a new version of the chapter or as a new version of the entire document. Only the application can determine whether versioning part of a compound object should version the whole. An application typically bases its versioning strategy on its desired extent of control over updates and its requirements for traceability of changes.

Some object DBMSs implement a new version of an object by making a copy of the object, assigning it a version number, and making appropriate entries in the version derivation graph. Another approach, sometimes called *versioning-by-difference*, is to record only the differences between the new version and its predecessor. This technique might be more appropriate when an application makes relatively minor changes to large objects, such as changing the border of a complex image. Versioning-by-difference, also known as *delta versioning*, can save considerable storage space, but it can increase the processing required to reconstitute an object and complicates the object DBMS's task of object management. Versioning-by-copy can be considered a form of the age-old technique of making backup copies of files.

An object DBMS must manage interobject references correctly when one or the other is versioned. Consider a customer object referenced by an order object, and vice versa. If an application changes the customer's address, it probably intends to update the customer object in place, with no versioning required. There is no need for the object DBMS to adjust interobject references. Consider now an order object referencing a product object, and vice versa. If an application changes the configuration or color or materials of the product object, it is possible that the application intends to create a new version of the object. The application then also must decide whether the order object should reference the old version or the new version of the product object.

In some cases, the latest version (i.e., the most recently created) of an object should always be referenced. In other cases, a specific version should be referenced, even if more recent versions exist. Some object DBMSs provide interfaces that enable programmers to specify version binding. An application can then work with a specific version of an object, or with multiple versions of the same object. Without this functionality, all applications typically bind to the latest version of every object.

Some object DBMSs go even further in supporting versioning semantics. For example, an application could mark a versioned object read-only, making it unchangeable. Enforcement by the object DBMS of such constraints could prevent unfortunate situations where some applications rely on the unchanging nature of a particular version of an object, but another application unknowingly changes the object.

IN CLOSING . . .

Thus there are a variety of approaches to making objects sharable, providing a range of options for coordinating updates. The conventional locking, logging, and two-phase commit protocols are transaction management techniques suitable for OLTP applications where updates must be highly synchronized. At the other end of the spectrum, multiversion concurrency control techniques allow independent updates to coexist indefinitely and are suitable for design and simulation applications. Object DBMS products support both conventional distributed transactions and multiversion concurrency control. Some are flexible enough to allow developers to fashion their own locking schemes and concurrency control protocols.

CHAPTER 9

Querying Objects

Object databases, like all other kinds of databases, need to be able to be accessed easily. Sometimes this is accomplished using the object programming language. Because of the close coupling of the object database and the object programming language, the application programmer accesses persistent and transient objects in a consistent way. The object programming language also serves as the database language because the programming language and the object database share a single type system, and because the object DBMS has been designed to use the programming language as an interface.

This is a particularly straightforward kind of interface for the object programmer to use. For example, the programmer simply uses the programming language syntax to find the value of an attribute of an object, as in finding the value of the `name` member of the vendor object pointed to by `v`:

```
vname = v->name;
```

There is no new database language to master. Similarly, the programming language supports following a reference or pointer when accessing one object from another, as in setting `v` to point to the vendor object whose address is stored in the `supplier` member of the object pointed to by `order`:

```
v = order->supplier;
```

This kind of access is based logically on a relationship that was specified in the class definitions for the two objects. `supplier` is the name of a traversal path from an order object to a corresponding vendor object.

APPLICATIONS SOMETIMES NEED VALUE-BASED ACCESS

However, not all object accesses are easily based on pointer traversals. There are times when applications need to be able to access objects based on characteristics other than their relationships. For example, an application might need to access all the vendors whose rating value is 1. The C++ language does not include any construct that easily and directly supports this value-based access. In C++, objects are accessed by supplying the appropriate reference or pointer.

Value-based access has historically been the domain of database query languages, the most famous of which is SQL [ANSI92] [Melt93]. Value-based accesses are usually simply called "queries." Chapter 5 reviewed some fundamental constructs of SQL.

Value-based access is useful for a wide variety of applications. One important use is to locate a starting point or anchor object in a database, from which the application will proceed to traverse through a network of other objects. The anchor might be the root of a compound document object, which the application could access by specifying the document number. The anchor might be the root of a part design. The starting point might be the object for a particular person, from which the application will traverse a genealogy. Most object DBMS products support a value-based query facility.

THE TERM "QUERY" IS USED INCONSISTENTLY

The database community uses the term "query" somewhat inconsistently. Sometimes people use the term to mean read-only access, as implied by the English word "inquiry." However, people commonly use "query" to mean any kind of declarative access. Declarative access, also known as non-procedural access, means that the programmer specifies what to return as a result, not how to find the result.

A major contribution of the researchers who developed SQL was a means for specifying declarative access to databases. Previous generations of DBMSs (e.g., IMS and the CODASYL systems) supported only procedural access. The programmer had to specify how to navigate the data structures that the DBMS used to implement the database. If a DBMS changed these data structures, then there was high probability that a programmer needed to change application code. It is undesirable for application code to depend on physical database structures. It is well accepted now that tuning or modifying physical database structures should never break applications.

Because SQL was intended to support declarative access in general, it provides not only read capability via the SELECT statement, but also statements for all other database actions, such as INSERT, DELETE, UPDATE, CREATE, DROP, COMMIT, ROLLBACK, and so forth. Because the acronym SQL means "Structured Query Language," the term "query" is often used to imply much more than read-only access. For now, we'll restrict our use of the term here to value-based access, which will omit transaction management, database opening and closing, and so forth. Discussion will focus on accessing objects based on their characteristics, which may be the values of their attributes, their connections via relationships, or the values resulting from execution of their operations.

THERE CAN BE MORE THAN ONE "STANDARD" OBJECT QUERY LANGUAGE

There is still considerable debate raging in the database community about the relative merits of a variety of proposed query languages for object databases. Object DBMS vendors have agreed on the semantics of a query language and a surface syntax, which has been published as ODMG-93 [Catt94]. The relational and extended-relational DBMS vendors are developing the semantics and syntax of the next generation of SQL [Melt94].

Because the pace of change in the area of object query languages is rapid, this chapter is not going to dwell on the syntax or semantics of any particular query language alternative. Some emphasis will be placed on the ODMG-93 query language, because it represents the agreement of the great majority of object DBMS vendors. The general philosophy of the ODMG is that it is appropriate for a variety of standard query language syntaxes to exist, with a common underlying semantics based on a well-specified object model. This chapter includes examples of a syntax for queries in C++, another syntax for queries in Smalltalk, and yet another SQL-like syntax. Each serves the needs of a particular kind of programmer.

The situation of multiple coexisting object query language syntaxes is quite different from that of the early days of relational DBMSs. Then there were two major query language camps: the SQL people and the QUEL people. The SQL camp was Oracle's domain, based on technology published by IBM researchers [Cham74]. The QUEL camp belonged to Ingres, based on technology published by researchers at the University of California, Berkeley [Ston76] [Ston85]. When DB2 came to market, IBM formally joined the SQL camp. SQL won the war, both in the marketplace and in the formal standards efforts. SQL and QUEL were not syntactic variants on a common semantic model. A relational DBMS engine could not support both. By contrast, an object DBMS can support a variety of surface syntaxes for the ODMG object query language semantics.

DATABASE PEOPLE EXPECT RICH QUERY LANGUAGE FEATURES

After their experiences with SQL, database people have developed expectations for the kinds of capabilities they should have available for querying object databases. Without these capabilities, the corresponding logic would need to be written into application programs in order to get the desired results. Expected features include the following:

- Quantification, which can be either existential (i.e., are there any objects that meet a specified search criterion?) or universal (i.e., for all the objects that meet a specified search criterion . . .). Of these two, the existential quantifiers, which are EXISTS in SQL, and its negation NOT EXISTS, are generally the more important.

- Operations on collections of objects and intermediate results. The programmer should not have to code intersections, unions, disjunctions, and so forth.

- Boolean functions, which allow simple search criteria to be combined logically into compound search criteria, using AND, OR, and NOT operations.

- Aggregate functions (e.g., COUNT, AVERAGE, MIN, MAX, SUM), which can be incorporated in the search criteria and in the specification of the target list.

- Sorting and grouping functions, which are used to order or group qualifying objects in particular ways according to the value of some common characteristic.

- Nested queries, or subqueries, which allow the results of one query to be used directly as the scope for the search criteria of another query.

Part of the controversy surrounding object query languages is how to mix programming language capabilities with the object DBMS responsibilities. For example, the ODMG 93 object query language semantics supports querying any type of object supported by the object programming language. A query may include operations defined on those types. For example, an age calculation might be executed as part of a query rather than in surrounding application code. If age is specified in C++ code, then the implication is that the object programming language must be freely intermixable with the query language.

Another controversy arises because the operations specified for classes are equally valid on both persistent and transient objects. This is quite different from the SQL-derivative perspective, where the DBMS provides the collection, boolean, aggregate, sorting, and grouping functions and the programming language provides other functions. There is a clear distinction that the programming language is used with transient data and SQL is used with persistent data. The SQL functions, including stored procedures, can execute only on persistent data, that is, they are database operations only. The programmer must continually be aware of the distinction between transient and persistent data. This distinction is one that the object DBMS products strive to remove.

THE OBJECT MODEL ALSO DICTATES FEATURES

An object query language is also expected to be consistent with and support the database's object model. This support has several aspects, as follows.

- A query should be able to specify any of a type's characteristics— attributes, relationships, and operations—in the query predicate and target list.

- A query should be able to execute polymorphic operations correctly on objects of classes and subclasses.

- Queries should range over objects of any type, regardless of whether they are transient or persistent.

There is not a lot of controversy around the first two aspects listed above. A concern that is sometimes voiced is whether querying attributes violate the principles of encapsulation. The response is typically that attributes should be implemented as C++ public `get_` and `set_` operations, not as data members. Querying by attribute value then implies that the corresponding operation is specified. For example, use the predicate

```
get_name() = "Joe"
```

rather than

```
name = "Joe"
```

The second aspect leverages late binding and polymorphism to enable simpler query specification. For example,

```
select e.pay_check_amount
    from e in Employees
```

executes a different implementation of the `pay_check_amount` operation for each subclass in the collection of `Employees`, such as `Hourly_employee` and `Salaried_employee`.

Database people and programming language people tend to be divided on their acceptance of the third point about whether queries should range over transient objects as well as persistent objects. In fact, some object DBMS products support query only of persistent objects, in the same way that the relational DBMS products restrict their scopes to database records only. It is not obvious which is the better approach. Querying transient objects introduces questions of scope. For example, if two CAD programs have each created transient objects of type Cube and one of them executes a query to find all the cubes in the upper-right quadrant and color them red, should the transient cubes from both programs be considered within the scope of the query? What if some of the cubes are from a design object that has been accessed from a database? Should only the persistent cubes on that object be colored red, or also the transient cubes introduced by the program? It is essential that the application programmer understand exactly the query semantics offered by the object DBMS.

QUERIES EXECUTE IN A VARIETY OF CONTEXTS

Queries may be issued not only within the context of application programs, but also interactively in a more ad-hoc fashion. The relational database approach has been that a single query language—SQL—should be used in all contexts. SQL is basically the same when embedded in FORTRAN, COBOL, C, C++, or used interactively. This characteristic of SQL is due in part to the philosophy that database records exist outside the context of any particular application or programming language. A relational database can be accessed from programs written in any of a variety of languages, using embedded SQL. The syntax and semantics of SQL are inseparable.

The result of the single query language philosophy is a certain degree of inevitable clash between the query language and its multiple host programming languages (see Fig. 9-1).

There are several points of evidence of these clashes. First there is a clear distinction between database variables and program variables. The programmer must explicitly copy values between these two kinds of variables, and the compiler and run-time system may or may not perform adequate type checking in those operations. Second, SQL has its own notions of expressions and functions, for example, the aggregate, boolean, sorting, and

FIGURE 9-1.
CLASHES BETWEEN SQL AND PROGRAMMING LANGUAGES [ATWO91].

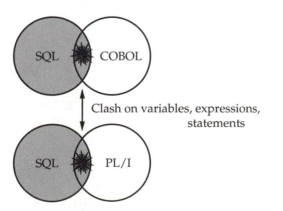

grouping functions listed earlier. The programmer cannot freely use these functions in programming language statements, nor can the programmer use programming language constructs in composing SQL statements.

Perhaps the most error-prone clash occurs because SQL implements a table model, which is not the same as the model supported by either the structured programming languages (FORTRAN, COBOL, C, etc.) or the object programming languages. The result of an SQL query is a table, which is basically a set of records. FORTRAN, COBOL, and C do not include appropriate constructs for manipulating tables. To handle this clash, SQL developers introduced the notion of *cursors*. A cursor is like a placeholder or iterator that is used by an application programmer to step one by one through the rows of a table. Thus, even though an SQL query returns a set (and is therefore sometimes called "set-oriented") into a database buffer area, the DBMS delivers the elements of the set to the application program one at a time.

The problem with these clashes is that the application programmer must design and code the logic to deal with the differences between the type systems of the programming language and SQL. This design and coding work can be error-prone and labor-intensive. In contrast, the object-oriented philosophy is to have the programming language and DBMS share the same type system, thereby obviating the need for the application programmer to deal with different type systems. An object DBMS therefore allows a C++ programmer to use C++ to query an object database. A Smalltalk programmer can use Smalltalk to query an object database. A COBOL programmer, who is already familiar with SQL, might prefer to use an SQL-derivative language to access an object database. If the object DBMS separates the syntax and semantics of the object query language, the language can have different syntaxes for different contexts. By supporting the semantics of the query language with multiple surface syntaxes, the object database could support C++, Smalltalk, and SQL-like queries to the same objects.

The object DBMSs available at this time do not quite achieve this multilingual access goal. Even if the object DBMS supports multiple object programming languages, it may not support multilingual access to a single collection of objects. In some cases, creating a persistent object using Smalltalk means that that object can be accessed only from Smalltalk, even if the object DBMS supports C++. Similarly, creating a persistent object using C++ may mean that the object can be accessed only from C++ or C.

QUERY LANGUAGE STYLES VARY WIDELY

A variety of object query languages have been proposed in the research literature. This chapter does not survey that work. Instead, we'll use examples of some representative object query languages to convey the basic principles of style and syntax variations.

There are two families of object query languages, each with its own objectives. We'll call the first family the *integrated family*. Its objective is seamless integration with host object programming languages. Members of this family are the object query languages supported by the object DBMS products that are closely coupled with object programming languages. We'll call the second family the *SQL family*. Its objective is leveraging SQL to accommodate object databases. Members of this family are the object query languages supported by relational DBMS products that have been extended to accommodate some aspects of objects. We've already discussed some of the differences between these families. Let's now look at some examples, starting with C++.

QUERIES CAN BE EXPRESSED IN STANDARD C++

Some members of the integrated family have the philosophy that no syntax should be added to C++ for any reason. The result of implementing this philosophy is that developers can use the object DBMS with any compiler that supports standard C++, and there is no need for preprocessors. Compatibility with standard compilers does not restrict customers' flexibility and choice in configuring their development environments. Avoiding preprocessors can make debugging programs easier.

One approach is for the object DBMS to support a function that takes a string containing the query as its argument. For example, the object DBMS could offer a `select` function to be inherited from a virtual base class. The `select` function could take as its argument a string form of the query predicate. For example:

```
Set<Vendor> top_vendors =
    Class<Vendor>.select(PAttribute("Vendor::rating()")==1);
```

In this case the query predicate applies to all objects in the `vendor` class, with the result being a set named `top_vendors` containing the qualifying instances of `vendor`.

This kind of interface looks quite natural to many experienced C++ programmers, but may be too subtle or complex for new C++ programmers and truly bizarre for SQL programmers. The same approach, however, could be used to appease the programmer familiar with SQL. For example:

```
SQL      mySQL;
mySQL.prepare ("SELECT * FROM VENDOR WHERE RATING=1");
SQLTable top_vendors = mySQL.execute();
```

This syntax looks quite natural to some SQL programmers but seems disruptive to many C++ programmers who would rather not see the SQL SELECT-FROM-WHERE syntax at all.

In either case, the query is actually phrased in standard C++. The SQL statements are coded as strings that C++ ignores.

QUERIES CAN BE EXPRESSED IN EXTENDED C++

Other members of the integrated family judge the seamlessness of the object database interface by how natural it is for the typical C++ programmer, rather than by how well it fits with a standard C++ compiler. The result has been extensions to C++ to accommodate query semantics, with careful attention paid to staying consistent with C++ style. This approach requires use of a preprocessor, which turns the introduced syntax into code that the compiler can understand. Vendors taking the extended C++ approach argue that the benefits of the easy-to-use interface and compile-time type checking outweigh the debugging complications the preprocessor introduces.

The example query from above could be phrased as follows:

```
set<Vendor*> top_vendors = vendors [rating()==1];
```

The object DBMS introduces the square-bracket syntax for specification of the predicate to be applied to a collection. In this example, the collection to be queried is named `vendors`. This syntax leverages the programmer's familiarity with C++ constructs for handling vectors. The syntax is a direct extension of the square-bracket syntax used in C++ to specify the index to be applied to a vector. For example, to access the third element of a vector named `rates`, the following C++ would be used:

```
int third_rate = rates [2];
```

Relationships can also be traversed using this kind of syntax. For example:

```
set<Vendor*> late_vendors =
     vendors [supplier_of [order_status=="late"]];
```

This query returns a set of pointers to `vendor` objects who are the suppliers of orders whose `order_status` attribute value indicates they are late. The `supplier_of` traversal path leads to a set of `order` objects, to which the innermost qualification criterion is applied.

This kind of interface does not meet the needs of the programmer who prefers to use SQL, but it is quite attractive to both relatively new and experienced C++ programmers. Because the query facility is easy to use, it is generally less error-prone than a more complex interface would be.

A side benefit of this approach is that queries can be posed against both persistent and transient objects using the same syntax. For example, the query above could be followed by another query:

```
set<Vendor*> late_vendors_in_Maine = late_vendors [state== "ME"];
```

The predicate syntax can be applied to any C++ collection.

QUERIES CAN BE SPECIFIED IN SMALLTALK

An object DBMS can provide query capability in Smalltalk using the `select` method that is already defined on Smalltalk collections. This approach implements a seamless interface that is natural to most Smalltalk programmers. Restating the examples from above:

```
topVendors :=
     Vendors allInstances select: [:v | v rating = 1].
```

```
lateVendors :=
    Vendors allInstances select: [:v | v supplier_of
        order_status = "late"].
lateVendorsInMaine :=
    lateVendors allInstances select [:v | state = "ME"].
```

SQL CAN BE EXTENDED FOR OBJECTS

The SQL family takes the approach of providing an object query language by extending SQL. Sometimes this means just retaining the SELECT-FROM-WHERE syntax, thereby maintaining upward compatibility with SQL and providing a smooth migration path to enable SQL-literate programmers to query object databases easily. This interpretation has been taken by some object DBMS vendors in their attempts to broaden the appeal of their products to the MIS marketplace. However, many of the relational DBMS vendors interpret "extending SQL" to mean adding capabilities to existing standard SQL. This is the direction adopted by the ANSI/ISO X3H2 SQL standardization committee.

There are several features that must be incorporated into SQL for accommodation of objects, including the following:

- **Object identifiers.** There is no equivalent concept in the relational model, as every row of every table is identified by a value-based primary key, not by a system-supplied identifier that is guaranteed to be unique for the life of the corresponding object, regardless of changes in the values of its characteristics.

- **Extensible data types.** SQL currently is restricted to operate on tables and SELECT statements always yield tables as results. These tables are basically sets, which do not allow duplicate elements. The elements are further constrained to be flat structures, that is, each field in a table row may only have a simple data type, e.g., integer, character, decimal, and so forth. A field may not have a more complex data type, like itself being a set. An object query language must be able to be applied to any type of data, and to yield appropriate object types as defined by the application.

- **Method invocation.** It must be possible for the query to specify operations in search predicates or target lists of SQL statements. SQL currently is restricted to using only database fields and some program variables in SQL statements.

- **Path expressions.** It must be possible for the query to specify that a relationship traversal path is to be navigated between objects. SQL currently is restricted to relating table rows only by comparing their values for specified fields and sometimes joining the related rows into a single new row.

- **Function specification.** Some relational DBMSs have already extended SQL to include specification of the logic of stored procedures. Either standard SQL needs to be extended to include this capability in a way that couples stored procedures with the pertinent type specification, or it must become possible to freely intermix SQL and programming language statements.

SQL appears to be evolving into a complete programming language. It will probably include capabilities for functions to be specified either in SQL, in an object programming language (notably C++), or in a conventional programming language. It will maintain its own type system, which will have to be interfaced by the application programmer with the programming language's type system.

Thus, extending SQL for objects will undoubtedly deliver capabilities for some relational DBMS products to support a much broader range of data types, which will be increasingly important to meet the growing need for media-rich applications. There is no conceptual reason why the object DBMSs and extended-relational DBMSs should not be able to support the same kinds of data types. The question will be whether the relational DBMS vendors can redesign and reimplement their underlying data structures and access methods to provide the same level of performance that the object DBMS vendors have been able to achieve with complex data types.

Extended-relational DBMSs may be able to deliver function-execution engines more quickly than the current object DBMS products can. Many of today's object DBMSs rely primarily on the object programming environment for function execution. An extended relational DBMS should be able to execute functions specified in SQL in the engine, outside the object programming environment. This capability may make it somewhat easier to implement large distributed object databases with many servers, where managing function code becomes a real challenge when code is replicated and distributed to a large number of application client machines.

As long as extensions to SQL maintain the notion of SQL having its own type system, it will not be possible to achieve the objective of seamless integration of the DBMS with the object programming language. The programmer will continue to provide the logic for mapping between the SQL type system and the object programming language type system, even if both support user-definable, extensible types. The value of seamless integration is simplicity, because the programmer needs to cope with fewer aspects of what can be a very complicated correspondence between type systems. One primary objective of object technology is to simplify inherently complex systems. This objective cannot be fully met if the programmer has to deal with one model for persistent objects and another model for transient objects.

ODMG OQL PROVIDES FOUNDATION QUERY SEMANTICS

ODMG-93 includes an object query language named OQL, which supports the ODMG object model. The ODMG-93 approach has been to describe the semantics of OQL with an abstract syntax, then to specify several alternative concrete syntaxes. These syntaxes enable OQL to take on the styles of C++, Smalltalk, or SQL. Operations that are defined on objects using C++ or Smalltalk (or some future computationally complete form of SQL) can be freely intermixed inside OQL statements. Update operations, transaction management, and so forth are programmed in the usual style of the object database-programming language combination.

OQL can be used to query any object whose type is defined to the object DBMS. The selection criteria can be based on the values of specified name attributes or the values of expressions phrased in the programming language. A query is essentially a function. The result is an object whose type may be inferred from the query expression. The result could be a subset of an existing database set, or new instances of existing types, or instances of new types. For example [Catt94]:

```
select distinct x.age
from x in Persons
where x.name = "Pat"
```

This is a query of the set of all objects of type `Person`, which are the elements of the extent named `Persons`. The query selects the ages of all persons named Pat. The query returns a literal of type `set<integer>`. In the following example, the query builds a structure containing `age` and `sex`. The result is a literal of type `set<struct>`.

```
select distinct struct(a: x.age, s: x.sex)
from x in Persons
where x.name = "Pat"
```

The next example shows a nested query.

```
select struct(a: x.age, s: x.sex)
from x in
    (select y from y in Employees where y.seniority="10")
        where x.name = "Pat"
```

The following example does not use the `select-from-where` construct. It simply returns the elements of the set named `Persons`:

```
Persons
```

The next example returns a set of parcel identifiers, for the parcels of land near the Skyline ridge, that have building plans whose maximum elevations are higher than the nearest point on the ridge line. It shows incorporation of specification of an operation (`is_near`), as well as use of relationship traversal paths:

```
select p.parcel_id
from p in Parcels, r in Ridges
where r.name = "Skyline"
    and p.location->is_near (r.ridge_line.location)
    and p.building_plans->maximum_elevation >
        r.location->nearest_point.elevation
```

The `is_near` operation is not specified in OQL, but rather in C++ or Smalltalk.

The SQL-like concrete syntax of OQL from [Catt94] has been used here. There are also chapters in [Catt94] that specify concrete syntaxes for queries in C++ and Smalltalk. The SQL-like syntax could be appropriate for use of

OQL in a stand-alone interactive mode, while the other concrete syntaxes are more appropriate for embedded use.

OBJECT DBMSs OPTIMIZE QUERIES

An object DBMS executes several steps to process a query, including:

- Parsing the query statement, checking its syntax and semantics, and recasting it into an internal representation, which is typically called a query graph.

- Deciding how to evaluate the query, based on availability of indexes, knowledge of data distributions and clusterings, knowledge of data volumes, and so forth.

- Constructing a set of candidate query plans, each of which specifies a sequence of low-level operations to be performed to run the query. A plan for a distributed query specifies where each low-level operation should run.

- Choosing the least expensive query plan.

These steps can all occur at compile time. The chosen plan is stored by the object DBMS and is used at runtime to guide execution of the query.

Not all object DBMSs offer the same level of optimization. Neither do the relational DBMS products. Some will show drastically different performance characteristics for two statements of the same query, differing only in the sequence of specification of the entries in a compound WHERE clause. The performance differences accrue because the DBMS generates two different query plans and is somehow dependent on the WHERE clause ordering. For example, consider the query to find the numbers of the orders with large quantities to be filled by suppliers in San Francisco. Here are two possible statements of the query:

```
SELECT o.order_no
FROM vendor v, order o
WHERE v.city = "SFO"
    AND o.supplier_name = v.vendor_name
    AND o.qty > 1000;

SELECT o.order_no
FROM vendor v, order o
```

```
WHERE o.qty > 1000
    AND v.city = "SFO"
    AND o.supplier_name= v.vendor_name;
```

Assume that there are 1,000,000 order records and 100 vendor records. The sequence of applying the qualification criteria will have significant impact on performance. A reasonable query optimizer will avoid joining a 1,000,000-row table by first applying the `o.qty>1000` predicate, producing a much smaller intermediate table that could be joined with the vendor table. The optimizer should build this query plan, regardless of the sequencing of predicates supplied by the programmer.

Query processing and optimization steps are basically the same for both object and relational databases. The difference is that the optimization becomes significantly more complex for object databases. The factors that contribute to this complexity include consideration of function invocations and path traversals, as well as inclusion of compound objects that must be configured from components that may be stored in clustered or distributed fashions. For example, it is difficult for the object DBMS to determine whether a function invocation is a short operation or a long operation without some understanding of the function's behavior and performance characteristics. If the operation is long, then the function should be executed on the fewest possible objects and the query plan should sequence low-level operations such that predicates are applied to filter out candidate objects before the function is invoked. However, if the function is a short operation, then it may not matter whether the nonqualifying objects are filtered out before the function invocation.

The unlimited scope of data types also complicates indexing, which is a well-understood way to improve query performance. No longer are conventional hash tables and B-tree indexes, which have served DBMSs well for numeric and character data, sufficient. For instance, other kinds of indexes, R-trees [Gutt84], must be introduced to handle spatial data.

IN CLOSING . . .

The object DBMS products in general do not yet offer query processing and optimization capabilities that are as advanced as those of some relational DBMSs. Some object DBMS vendors, however, already have query facilities that are even more powerful than existing SQL. In keeping with the object database philosophy of seamless integration with the programming language environment, there will be a variety of standard query syntaxes for object databases, with powerful underlying query language semantics that the object DBMS vendors have agreed to support. Programmers will phrase queries differently in C++, Smalltalk, and stand-alone mode. SQL will continue to be a major influence, as it is extended and modified to incorporate object principles.

CHAPTER 10

Evaluating Object DBMSs

Selecting an object DBMS product is an important process. Like any other successful data management technology, the product selected today begins to define the legacy of the future. There are many different parameters that can be used to evaluate the object DBMS alternatives, and there is no single most-correct process for conducting an evaluation. Not only are there many possible pertinent evaluation criteria, but there also is typically a degree of uncertainty about the requirements and characteristics of the target application environment. This chapter focuses on evaluation criteria, with emphasis on object database performance.

EVALUATORS APPLY MANY CRITERIA

The list of criteria applied to judge object DBMS products are generally the same as those used to evaluate relational DBMSs and software packages in general. Factors that are typically considered include the following:

- Performance—How fast is the product?

- Scalability—How well does the product perform as the size of the system grows?

- Functionality—What features does the product offer?

- Usability—How easy is it to use the product?

- Reliability—How often does the product fail?

- Support—How responsive is the vendor in providing help?

- Environment—Does the product run in the target computing system?

- Viability—How likely is it that the vendor will be in business in the future?

• Price—What does the product cost, both in the short term and over its expected lifetime?

Each of these factors includes more detailed factors. The pertinent factors are those that lead to a well-reasoned conclusion about how closely the product meets the requirements of the intended application environment, characterized in its entirety to include all aspects of user needs, budgets, hardware/software/staffing constraints, and so forth.

Performance is typically one of the top evaluation criteria for data management software. Because the object DBMS products are still relatively new, many customers expect that the vendors will continue over time to improve functionality, usability, reliability, and support. They are willing to accept products that may not entirely meet their wish-list specifications in these areas. However, they typically do want to get the best performance possible. An end-user's level of satisfaction with an application is largely determined by that application's performance. If the end-users are not happy, the developers are not happy. DBMS performance can be a significant factor in determining the application's performance.

BENCHMARKS PREDICT PERFORMANCE

Because performance is so important, many organizations would like to be able to predict the performance of an object DBMS product on their applications prior to actually implementing the applications or even purchasing the object DBMS product. Predicting performance involves determining how the object database will perform given the particular characteristics of the applications and their environment. A typical approach to predicting DBMS performance is to use a benchmark, which is representative of the application workload without actually being a replica of that application.

Developing a good benchmark can be extremely difficult, depending on the complexity of the intended application and how closely the benchmark is intended to match the application workload. Some organizations decide that it is worthwhile to develop benchmarks that fairly closely represent their applications. Other organizations decide that it is sufficient to base their evaluations on candidate products' performance on published benchmarks. Either approach can be effective, as long as the organization understands (1) the cost of developing truly representative benchmarks, and (2) the limitations of benchmarks that are not necessarily representative.

THOROUGH BENCHMARKS ARE COMPLEX

Assume that a benchmark has been identified or developed that sufficiently represents the characteristics of the application. Evaluators could study many metrics to compare the performance of candidate object DBMS products. Some of these metrics include the following:

Access times

- Time to access an object from persistent storage

- Time to access a persistent object that is already in program memory

- Time to create a new object in persistent storage

- Time to load a database with a group of objects

- Time to access a group of objects from persistent storage

- Time to lock an object

Response times

- Time to respond to a given set of transactions

Throughput

- Number of transactions that can be completed in a given period

Storage

- Storage overhead associated with a single persistent object

- Storage requirements for a group of objects

- Program-memory overhead associated with a single persistent object

- Storage requirements for logs

- Memory requirements for the runtime DBMS

A thorough benchmark would typically report some or all of these factors measured under a variety of circumstances. For example:

- With logging and without logging. Logging introduces additional accesses to persistent storage and can significantly affect both response times and throughputs.

- With locally stored databases and with remotely stored databases. Accessing remote databases via network linkages can introduce significant time delays and potential bottlenecks, depending on the characteristics of the network and accesses. Some object DBMSs use anticipatory client-side caching techniques that improve their performance with remote databases.

- With small databases and with large databases. Measuring database performance with larger volumes can help assess whether the object database will scale well.

- With small objects and with large objects. Some object DBMSs are better tuned for fine-grained objects than for coarse-grained objects, and vice versa.

- With a single user and with multiple users. Object contention and the effects of locking to control sharability become evident only with multiple users.

- In homogeneous and heterogeneous systems. Object DBMSs typically incur extra processing requirements if they need to translate object representations across different computer architectures.

The characteristics of the intended application environment should guide selection of the pertinent set of conditions to be included in a suite of benchmarks. For example, if the applications will always run in single-user mode on a desktop machine, then it is unnecessary to include variations to evaluate how the candidate object DBMSs handle locking and heterogeneity. If the applications are designed with only coarse-grained objects, then it may be unnecessary to evaluate performance of the candidate object DBMSs with fine-grained objects. Part of the challenge here is to anticipate future application requirements as well as characterize current requirements.

RELATIONAL DBMS BENCHMARKS TYPICALLY CHARACTERIZE OLTP APPLICATIONS

The relational DBMS community has expended considerable energy in the design and standardization of benchmarks to help customers evaluate DBMSs. Among the most important efforts in this area have been those of the Transaction Processing Council (TPC), a consortium of vendors who have precisely defined benchmarks for database transaction processing applications. These benchmarks are intended to be representative of a large class of on-line transaction processing (OLTP) applications for which relational DBMSs are commonly deployed [TPC89].

One of the TPC benchmarks is called *TPC-A*. This benchmark is based on a debit/credit benchmark characterizing simple update transactions against a database. The database has three tables: a customer account table containing a balance for each account, a teller table containing a balance for each teller, and a branch table containing a balance for each branch of the bank. Another table contains a history of completed transactions. A transaction includes the following steps:

- Receive a message from a teller.

- Begin a new transaction.

- Update the account table.

- Update the teller table.

- Update the branch table.

- Insert a record into the history table.

- End the transaction.

- Respond to the teller.

The metric recorded is throughput in transactions per second. TPC-A includes rigorous specifications governing how to run the benchmark. Representative requirements are as follows:

- System properties, which must be in effect during the transaction. These are called the ACID properties: Atomicity, Consistency, Isolation, and Durability. The DBMS must ensure *atomicity* during the benchmark, so that no partial transactions are permitted to modify the database. The DBMS must support *consistency* during the benchmark by ensuring that each transaction takes the database from one consistent state to another. The DBMS must ensure *isolation*, also known as serializability, of all transactions during the benchmark, so that the results of concurrently executing transactions are the same as the results that would have been achieved by some serial execution of the transactions. Finally, the DBMS must ensure *durability* by preserving the effects of all committed transactions even if there are system or media failures.

- Table layouts, number of records for each table, and the minimum number of rows of each table that must be accessed per test.

- Rules for distributing and partitioning data among tables, for timing transactions, and for configuring hardware for the tests.

- Requirements and recommendations for reporting benchmark activity and results so that the tests can be repeated by independent parties. This information is used in auditing vendors' benchmark implementations.

TPC-A includes simulation of many users, their "think time," and network traffic times. A variant on TPC-A, called *TPC-B*, removes consideration of think time.

The TPC benchmarks are representative of OLTP workloads, which are characteristic of many relational DBMS applications. Nearly all relational DBMS vendors publish their products' performance on these benchmarks. There are no known published reports of object database performance on the TPC benchmarks. However, it is highly likely that today's object DBMS products would not perform as well as the relational DBMSs. This is partly due to the fact that the relational vendors typically have devoted substantial resources to tuning their products to excel in OLTP applications, while the object DBMS vendors have not. However, there is no obvious technical reason why the object DBMSs could not perform as well as the relational DBMSs on the TPC benchmarks, given sufficient timing and incorporation of optimization technology. There are not many cases where object databases are used to support OLTP applications today, and this is not a target market for the technology. Object databases are used to support applications that differ substantially from OLTP.

ENGINEERING BENCHMARKS BETTER CHARACTERIZE OBJECT DATABASE APPLICATIONS

The early applications of object DBMSs were primarily in engineering applications, especially computer-aided design. The data management requirements for these applications differ from OLTP in several fundamental ways, including the following:

- Few large transactions versus many small transactions. Typical design applications have logical units of work that run for minutes, hours, or days, rather than for milliseconds.

- Complex operations versus simple queries. Typical design applications operate on a relatively large but unchanging collection of related objects, traversing among them and executing complex operations. By contrast, OLTP involves simple single-record accesses into tables and sometimes does not even involve joining across tables.

- Client–server architectures versus central-server architectures. Typical design applications are both data- and compute-intensive and take advantage of desktop workstation capabilities with a substantial amount of the processing run in the client, accessing objects that may be stored persistently at potentially many server sites in a network. By contrast, OLTP assumes that the database processing runs primarily on a single server.

Several benchmarks have been developed to better reflect the characteristics of applications that benefit from object database capabilities. The two best known of these benchmarks are the Engineering Database Benchmark (also called 001, the Sun Benchmark, or the Cattell Benchmark), developed at Sun Microsystems [Catt92], and 007, developed at the University of Wisconsin [Care94].

The Engineering Database Benchmark was intended to prove or disprove two hypotheses: (1) that an object DBMS can achieve better raw performance than a relational DBMS for engineering operations by a factor of 10 to 100, and (2) that certain characteristics common to object DBMS architectures are responsible for the difference. Of particular interest were object DBMSs' client-side caches and efficient access to remotely stored objects.

In addition to reporting a single weighted metric, the Engineering Database Benchmark measures performance for several operations, including:

- Creating a database consisting of 20,000 parts and 60,000 interconnections

- Selecting 1000 part identifiers at random, retrieving the parts with those identifiers, and performing an operation on each

- Selecting one part at random, traversing all connections from it to other parts in a depth-first manner to seven levels, and performing an operation on each

- Executing the same traversal in reverse order, starting with a randomly selected part and retrieving all the parts connected to it, and so forth

- Entering 100 new parts and 3 connections from each to other randomly selected parts, then committing the updates.

The benchmark executes operations with the application code and database located on a single machine, then again with them located on two different machines. Results are recorded for both a "cold start," where the database existed only on disk and no objects are already cached in memory, and a "warm start," after ten iterations of each operation, so that many objects are already cached. The benchmark requires only single-user access and does not measure performance with sharing or contention for objects.

This benchmark has been run for many of the object DBMS products. However, some of the results are available only for relatively early releases of those products. Results [Catt92] show that the measured object DBMSs were 30 or more times faster than the benchmarked relational DBMS.

The 007 benchmark characterizes a broader mix of operations and measures object DBMS performance with multiuser access. Over 100 metrics are reported. Benchmark implementations are audited by the University of Wisconsin and results are available from participating object DBMS vendors.

An obvious question is whether these published benchmark results are of value in your evaluation of candidate object DBMS products. The answer is largely dependent upon how well the characteristics of the benchmark match the characteristics of your applications. A benchmark can be an accurate predictor of performance only to the extent that it reflects the application. If a benchmark is unrepresentative, then developers can be misled by basing product evaluation on the benchmark results.

Determining whether a benchmark reflects the characteristics of an application requires understanding a variety of factors about the application. Some of these factors include the following:

- Mix of kinds of access, for example, value-based access versus traversal, highly predictable versus unpredictable, retrieval versus update

- Network configuration and distribution of objects among nodes

- Transaction durations, complexities, and scope of object-access requirements

- Number of concurrent users and probability of contention for shared objects

- Database and object sizes

- Patterns of growth and dynamics of access.

Many customers who develop benchmarks do not construct extensive benchmarks that faithfully reflect detailed understanding of their applications. Some select what they consider to be the most important kinds of access, write a somewhat simplistic benchmark to reflect the characteristics of those accesses, and evaluate the performance of candidate object DBMS products based on that benchmark.

Many customers decide not to benchmark more than one object DBMS product, but rather apply benchmarking after they have chosen a leading candidate based on weighing other factors. The benchmark results are used to make a go or no-go decision based on whether the leading candidate can deliver a certain expected level of performance. This approach can be considerably less costly and time-consuming than implementing a benchmark for multiple object DBMS products and comparing their performance.

THERE ARE MANY SOURCES OF PRODUCT INFORMATION

There are many sources of information about object DBMS products, including

- vendors

- consultants

- feature reports

- customers.

Many vendors participate in various trade conferences and exhibits. They make product literature available, give demonstrations, and have people available who will be delighted to tell you how the products are differentiated from each other. There is a growing number of consultants with substantial expertise in evaluation and use of object DBMS products. Some are independents; others are with large consulting firms. There are also reports available that compare object DBMS products on a feature-by-feature basis. One of the more extensive is [Barr94].

Some of the most reliable sources of information about object DBMS products are the customers who are using them to develop and deploy real applications. Most object DBMS vendors make available contact information about reference accounts. Some customers speak about their experiences at the various trade conferences.

IN CLOSING . . .

There is another area related to performance that is not typically measured by benchmarks but should be considered when evaluating object

DBMS products. One of the reasons that organizations adopt object technology is to improve programmer productivity and the extensibility and adaptability of their applications. Related factors that may prove important in an evaluation include:

- seamlessness of the programming language interface

- extent of the vendor's support group's expertise in your industry or application area

- availability of application development tools

- availability of object modeling tools that generate class specification code

- availability of low-level foundation classes for a variety of data structures and algorithms

- availability of browsers and debuggers that consistently handle both transient and persistent objects.

CHAPTER 11

Directions

We've seen that object database technology offers functionality to satisfy both the object programmer and the database manager. The object programmer expects high-performance persistent storage management from a nearly invisible database. The object database should slip into the object programming environment in a way that allows the programmer to continue with familiar conventions. As a side benefit, the objects in the database become sharable and can be distributed without the programmer having to do anything special.

The database manager expects the object DBMS to offer conventional DBMS functionality (transactions, concurrency control, schema management, query processing, and so forth) without the constraints of the relational table model. The object DBMS stores and manages objects, which means the database can easily handle "unconventional," that is, nontabular, data types—text, graphics, images, voice, video, blobs, and so forth—and highly interrelated data—networks, bills-of-materials, geometries, time series, and so on.

In addition to providing database management support for a broad range of data, object databases are well suited for applications to be deployed in distributed computing environments. Vendors developed the object DBMS products during the workstation era with heavy influence from customers who were to deploy their applications in networks. Thus the products incorporate substantial distributed functionality. They support distributed transactions and provide features for collaborative, workgroup applications.

We've also seen that an object DBMS is an integrated member of the family of object technologies. Developers can use object models to design object class libraries and database schemas, with the type system shared between the object database and programming language environments. The synergy between the object technologies leads to simplified application development and maintenance. We've seen examples of the reduction in application complexity that results when the object programmer uses C++ with an object database rather than a relational database.

Now let's consider the market for object DBMS products and directions for development of object DBMS technology.

THIS IS A GROWTH MARKET

A typical way to forecast a technical market is with optimism for continual growth, resulting in revenues that at least double annually for the major players and that grow much faster than that for a few lucky ones. Industry watchers in the late 1980s expected the market for object DBMSs to grow dramatically.

The object database market is a small fraction of the overall database business. In 1991 the general DBMS market was approximately $4.12 billion; the object DBMS portion of that was about $10 million [DeAr91], which is roughly .24 percent of the overall database market. However, the growth rate of the object DBMS market was considerably greater than that of the relational market. In 1992 the relational market was growing about 17 percent annually, while the object DBMS growth rate was near 350 percent [IDC92]. There were projections in 1990 that the 1993 market for object DBMSs would be $153 million [Jeff90]. In reality, the worldwide revenues for 1992 were about $40 million and for 1993 were about $60 million. While these numbers are nowhere near optimistic projections, they still represent a healthy, growing market. In fact, the object database market is maturing at about the same rate as the relational database market did at the comparable stage in the early 1980s.

The buyers for object DBMS products through 1993 were primarily OEMs (original equipment manufacturers) and VARs (value-added resellers). The OEMs are the large-systems vendors. Some are reselling object DBMS products. There has also been substantial adoption of object databases as the basis for applications in the CAD and CASE arenas, with telecommunications and financial systems following close behind.

In addition to demand from these application areas, the growth of the object database market to date has been fueled by various factors in the computer industry at large:

- Object technology in general is gaining broader acceptance, and object DBMS products today specifically depend on acceptance of object programming languages. Objects appear to be the most promising software development advance of the decade, if not the most hyped. At the beginning of the 1990s it was rare to find mention of object technology at trade shows targeted at CASE, mainstream database, or software for particular vertical markets; today, however, trade shows feature a great number of product descriptions and speakers address topics related to object technology.

- Distributed computing is becoming more widespread. Object DBMS products today execute primarily in networked UNIX workstation and server environments, with growing availability on PCs. The downsizing trend and prevalence of LANs provide opportunity for the object DBMS vendors.

- Some hardware vendors are making a "buy" decision relative to object DBMSs, rather than building their own products from scratch. This of course increases the business of the object DBMS vendors whose products are selected by the hardware vendors.

The object DBMS products are also maturing, making them suitable as engines for production applications. As of this writing, many of the products are in their third major releases, with consequent improvements in quality and functionality from the earlier market situation. The products are available on a wide range of platforms, and standards are being established, such as [Catt94].

THE ODBMS VENDORS HAVE LARGE CHALLENGES AHEAD OF THEM

An interesting and applicable model of market growth for high-technology products such as object DBMSs is excellently portrayed in Geoffrey Moore's book, *Crossing the Chasm* [Moor91]. The author describes the usual stages of growth: innovators, early adopters, early majority, late majority, and laggards. He then introduces a rather formidable chasm between the early adopters and the early majority (see Fig. 11-1).

In my opinion, the object DBMS market of the mid-1990s sits firmly in the chasm. The vendors in the chasm must figure out how to make their technology products appeal to the broader marketplace, which has different expectations and risk-taking profiles than the early adopters.

The first market for a new product area like object DBMS is innovators, who buy product because it is new technology. Many of these buyers are in advanced technology departments in large companies; others are in academics. The purchase is typically for one or two development copies, which are either used in particular experimental projects or made available in a laboratory for whoever may want to try them. The buyers' objectives are to learn about the technology and determine whether or not it is real.

Early adopters buy technology products because they meet certain specific needs and enable buyers to do new things. Object DBMS sales to early adopters are commonly to small project teams that are building prototype systems. Like the innovators, early adopters of object DBMSs are willing to cobble together their own development environments. They take what they perceive to be the best product offerings in the pertinent categories—for example, object DBMS plus object programming language compiler plus application development tools plus GUI libraries plus network perfor-

FIGURE 11-1.
MARKET MATURATION MODEL FROM *CROSSING THE CHASM* **[MOOR91].**

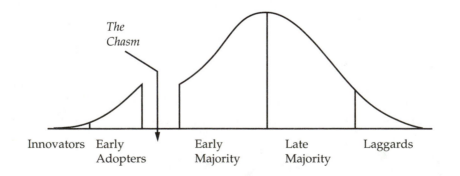

mance analysis tools—and integrate them for their own purposes. The project team may seek help from a third-party expert consultant and may rely on the testimony of innovators to substantiate the viability of their prototype projects. The team typically expects that if the system is successful, the prototype will show substantial value and be moved into a production development environment.

In contrast, the early majority (and even more so the late majority) is considerably more adverse to taking risks. These people commonly do not want to learn to use a new object database technology and a new programming language and a new development methodology, all at the same time. These buyers want technology products to fit easily into their existing computing environments, without substantial learning curves or integration efforts. The members of the early majority are typically willing to use new products that enable them to improve what they're already doing. They are commonly adverse to taking the risk of doing things differently.

The early majority has the potential to use object databases as the foundation for "mainstream," or widely deployed, applications. Many object DBMS vendors have pricing policies that distinguish between development and runtime licenses. Most vendors do not make much profit from development copies, primarily due to the costs of supporting customers who are actively using the products to develop applications. The vendors plan to make their fortunes through the sale of runtime licenses. The model is typically that a successful development-license sale will mature into the sale of 10 to 1000 runtime licenses. The object DBMS products must be embedded as runtime engines in mainstream applications in order for object DBMS vendors to have viable businesses. It will be interesting to see what happens to the object DBMS pricing models as object operating systems incorporate object DBMSs into their kernels.

To cross the chasm, object DBMS vendors have to position their products to appeal to the risk-taking profiles and product requirements of the early majority. Many object DBMS vendors today position their products with statements such as "Our object DBMS will enable you to tackle applications that never before were possible." The message is that the object DBMS will help ensure success with innovative, new applications. The technology is part of a new way of doing things. In fact, the tendency is to proclaim that object technology revolutionizes the way that software is developed. This is not exactly the message that typically appeals to the more risk-adverse early majority. This market segment basically wants a better way of doing whatever they're already doing. They want evolution, not revolution.

To cross the chasm, object DBMS vendors must also face a variety of technical challenges:

- Object DBMSs must become part of "whole product" offerings. Smoothly integrated tools and highly effective consulting services must be available to facilitate use of object databases in large-scale software development projects.

- There must be straightforward, easily understood processes for integrating object databases and their applications with existing nonobject-oriented systems and databases.

- The programming languages used with object databases must be acceptable to the computing community at large.

- Standards for application portability across object databases must be established and supported by object DBMS vendors.

- Object databases must prove to be scalable. They must be able to support very large volumes of data with many concurrent users.

- There must be substantial, published accounts of success with object DBMS products and credible references within each of the target vertical market segments.

All these challenges are currently being addressed by the object DBMS vendors and their partners. Let's consider these points in more detail.

OBJECT DBMSs MUST BE PART OF "WHOLE PRODUCT" OFFERINGS

One of the developments that will greatly enhance the movement of the object databases into the early majority markets will be the availability of smoothly integrated companion tools. The relational DBMS products encountered the need for this transition as well.

Initially, relational buyers were content to buy relational DBMS engines. They were early adopters who were using relational technology because there was no other way for them to meet their application requirements. As the relational DBMS engines became more widely used, an aftermarket for relational tools was established. These tools included forms packages, report writers, data dictionaries, fourth-generation languages (4GLs), and so forth. The availability of these tools made it easier for people to develop and maintain relational database applications.

The most successful relational DBMS vendors offer not just their engines, commonly called their "servers," but also a variety of tools. A relational vendor's tools products typically account for about 25 percent of its revenues. Many relational vendors are still investing heavily in the development of tools suites intended to make application developers more effective. There is also a lively market for DBMS-independent tools from independent vendors. Tools to accompany object DBMSs are beginning to appear on the market as of this writing and should accelerate the adoption of object DBMS products.

The adoption rates of C++ and Smalltalk, and therefore also of the object databases for C++ and Smalltalk, have been aided by the availability of integrated object programming environments. Customers want to be able to use the same class library browsers and debuggers, whether or not an object database is involved.

Object modeling tools also help the adoption rate of object databases. The ability to design a class library and have a tool generate the bulk of the code necessary for the object database schema facilitates the use of object DBMS technology by the early majority.

The object DBMS vendors are also in the process of developing improved object database administration tools. These tools will simplify installation of object DBMSs and object database applications, especially in distributed computing environments. They will make it easier to monitor the performance of object databases and tune their configurations. They will enable system administrators to track and manage an object DBMS's interactions with transaction management products and operating systems.

Another important aspect of an object DBMS "whole product" offering is the availability of knowledgeable consulting services to help early adopter customers be successful in their use of the technology. It will not suffice for the object DBMS vendors to develop their own consulting services organizations. These services must be readily available from independent sources, including both small consulting firms and the large-systems integrators and consulting houses. The presence of this expertise will be an indicator of the success of the object DBMS vendors in crossing their chasm. Clearly, there is a bit of a chicken-and-the-egg phenomenon here.

OBJECT DATABASES MUST BE INTEGRATED WITH THE LEGACY

The early majority will also require that object databases be easily integrated with the legacy of other technologies in their computing environments. Some of this need is being addressed by the vendors who provide gateway tools from the object programming languages to relational DBMSs. Many customers also need commercial gateways to IMS and the legacy of network DBMSs.

Early majority customers who want to mix object databases and relational systems will request transaction management capabilities that cross object and relational DBMS boundaries. Applications that access both object and relational databases will need assurance that transaction commits are coordinated across both sources of persistence. The relational vendors have together developed standards for heterogeneous, distributed database access. These standards will be extended to incorporate object database access, helping to ensure the viability of transactions that mix technologies.

Some early majority customers and many late majority customers will want the details of what data are stored in which databases to be completely invisible to the application programmer. They will want to write applications to access a logical database that may be implemented physically as a mix of one or more object databases and one or more relational databases. These programmers will expect automatic intermodel mapping support and mixed-model transactions.

OBJECT DATABASES MUST BE ACCESSIBLE FROM MAINSTREAM PROGRAMMING LANGUAGES

The use of object programming languages, notably C++ and Smalltalk, is growing rapidly, as their vendors successfully cross their own chasms.

Moving from the early adopters to the early majority is easier for the C++ vendors than for the Smalltalk vendors. C++ can be sold to the C programmer as a better C; this is a message that appeals to the risk profile of the early majority. C++ enables C programmers to do what they already do, only better. In contrast, Smalltalk does not represent an incremental step from any other programming language. There's been some suggestion that Smalltalk should be marketed as a 4GL for the MIS marketplace, rather than as an object programming language. Many MIS developers have already accepted 4GLs as a relatively effective productivity tool for application development. Packaged with the appropriate class libraries, Smalltalk might be accepted as an incremental improvement on the 4GLs of the early 1990s.

Many object DBMS vendors do not want to wait for the object programming languages to be embraced by the early majority before they can leap the chasm. For the most part, the object DBMS products of the mid-1990s will continue to depend on either a C++ or a Smalltalk interface. The early adopters of object databases have been happy to learn an object programming language. However, moving object databases into the mass market requires interfaces to the programming languages used by the majority of programmers, notably COBOL, SQL, and probably Ada and BASIC. It is highly unlikely that large numbers of COBOL and SQL programmers will quickly metamorphose into C++ programmers.

Considerable effort has already been expended in making object extensions to both COBOL [ANSI93] [Topp94] and SQL [Melt94]. Some object DBMSs will provide interfaces for OOCOBOL and Object SQL. Others may gain market share by interfacing with COBOL and SQL regardless of whether they include object extensions.

OBJECT DBMS STANDARDS MUST BE ESTABLISHED AND SUPPORTED

Software standards are important for several reasons. From a marketing perspective they are important because they represent the maturing of the technology and a safe-buy signal to prospective buyers. From a technical perspective they are important because they are essential to application portability and interoperability.

Software standards are developed in three major ways. The first is the formal route, where standards are developed by committee efforts through the sanctioned standards-setting bodies, including the American National Standards Institute (ANSI) and the International Standards Organization (ISO). The second is through industry coalitions of companies that have a shared vested interest in standards for their product lines. The third is through market share, where the vendor whose product captures the lion's share of the market sets de facto standards.

All three of these types of standards development are underway today with object database technology. The bulk of the formal effort is coming from ANSI X3H2, which is the SQL committee and its companion ISO committees. As mentioned several times, ANSI X3H2 is investigating object extensions to SQL [Melt94]. Under consideration are extensions to enable developers to define abstract data types, to define type–subtype hierarchies, to invoke procedures from within SQL statements, to define intertype relationships, and so forth. There is also discussion of making SQL into a computationally complete, object-oriented programming language. ANSI X3H2 published a standards specification at the end of 1992 and can publish no more frequently than at three-year intervals.

A consortium of the object DBMS vendors, known as the Object Database Management Group (ODMG), developed the first standard specifically addressing object database technology. ODMG was formed in the summer of 1991 as an independent organization to propose and promote standards for object databases. The group focused its efforts on the definition of common database interfaces that the involved companies' respective object DBMS products will support. ODMG-93 [Catt94] includes specification of an object model defining a standard for the semantics of database objects, an object definition language (ODL) that is independent of any programming language, an object query language (OQL), and standard interfaces for C++ and Smalltalk.

In 1989 a coalition of companies interested in establishing standards that would help ensure the interoperability of software products developed by different vendors formed the Object Management Group (OMG). Object database technology is also somewhat related to the standards being adopted by the OMG. OMG uses object technology as the basis for achieving interoperability. The components of an OMG-conformant computing environment include

- Object request broker (ORB)—responsible for dispatching and delivering messages between objects, no matter where they reside on a network.

- Object services—include facilities for object naming, object creation and deletion, object persistence, transaction management, concurrency control, event notification, replication management, and so forth.

- Common objects—used by many applications and include print facilities, editors, compilers, debuggers, and so forth.

- Application objects—provide application-specific functionality.

An object database can be considered to be an object that provides integrated object services functionality. Thus, for certain environments that adopt the OMG perspective, it will be important for object DBMS products to support the standards that the OMG adopts for object services. A major difference between the object DBMS and OMG object services approaches is the integration of services and the consequent performance offered by the object DBMSs.

OBJECT DATABASES MUST PROVE TO BE SCALABLE

For adoption by the early majority, the object DBMS products must prove to be scalable. They must be able to support large numbers of users, with large databases. Potential adopters must feel comfortable that selected object DBMSs will be able to support their application needs as those application environments grow.

Certain features of object DBMSs directly address the scalability issue. For example, some object DBMSs support the movement of objects across storage volumes located either at the same site or at different sites, with no disruption to application code. Some object DBMSs support archiving, which allows portions of object databases to be moved to off-line storage but to remain available when applications need to access archived objects. An object database that supports distributed queries (i.e., queries that involve objects at multiple sites) is likely to be more scalable than one that requires that all objects involved in a query reside at a single site. The distributed capability allows applications to evolve gracefully from single-site, single-user mode to multisite, multiuser mode.

Scalability also requires functionality that enables an object database to support continuously operating applications, that is, 24-hour, 7-day availability. This requirement means that a scalable object database must support on-line backup with both roll-forward and roll-back capabilities.

Some large-scale deployments will use replication of objects to ensure that applications can achieve their performance and availability requirements. A replicated object is one for which there are at least two copies, which the object DBMS synchronizes to remain equal. Chapter 7 addressed some issues involved in managing replicated objects. Replication is especially useful in applications that are deployed over wide-area networks.

SUCCESS STORIES MUST BE REFERENCEABLE

Finally, it is typical for early majority buyers to make purchase decisions based in part on access to other buyers' use of the technology. To be credible, buyers must consider these references to be in situations similar to their own. References are most credible if they highlight use of the object databases in a similar application in an organization of similar size using a similar computing environment.

Having referenceable success stories is one of the reasons that technology vendors sometimes focus on particular vertical markets. For example, some of the great success that Sybase had in establishing itself as a relational DBMS vendor in an already-crowded field was due to its early focus on Wall Street financial firms. The Sybase product met the needs of this market segment, and each sale became a potential reference for additional sales. After establishing a firm foothold in this market segment, Sybase was able to branch successfully into other segments. The company established its positioning as a technology vendor, not as a niche vendor interested only in supporting financial applications.

The object DBMS vendors are working hard to make their customers successful and to cultivate referenceable success stories. Not all successful customers turn into reference accounts. For example, a customer deploying object technology and object databases to gain competitive advantage may well want to keep the activity confidential and under nondisclosure.

THE MARKET IS CHANGING RAPIDLY

Object DBMS products are evolving relatively rapidly, adding to the existing marketplace confusion. Object DBMS products are sprouting SQL-like interfaces, and some may soon support conventional programming languages. Relational vendors are developing hybrid products that support both the relational and object models. Some will not only offer object extensions to SQL, but also interfaces to the object programming languages. The boundaries between the product family categories are blurring. Confusion enters in part because there are no answers to questions such as:

- How much object-orientedness does an extended-relational DBMS need to qualify as an object DBMS?

- How much does the kernel of a relational DBMS have to change to qualify as a pure object DBMS?

- How much SQL does a pure object DBMS need to qualify as providing the familiarity advantages of an extended-relational system?

There are numerous object DBMS vendors today. Some industry watchers think there may be too many and that the mid-1990s will be a period of merger-and-acquisition activity, sprinkled with several company failures. Others, however, point out that the relational DBMS market did not go through its consolidation period to today's handful of dominant players until after the field had broadened to include more than 40 vendors. Perhaps the object DBMS market will similarly mushroom before it reaches a mature state.

Object database technology will continue to provide a rich area for innovation for many years. Some of the research and development areas include

- High availability—with no planned downtime at all

- Storage hierarchies—heuristics and algorithms for anticipating movement between levels of storage

- Tool integration—leading to specification-driven implementation and maintenance

- Interoperability—so that a single object database can efficiently support multiple object programming languages, with seamless integration to all

- Rules and constraints—to enhance the semantics of object databases

- Execution servers—making object databases active managers of operations as well as data structures

- Security—providing certifiable levels of protection and other, more flexible, schemes of authorization

- Legacy integration—hiding all details of physical access through a common unified logical object model

- Interfaces—leading to much higher level "languages" or approaches to specifying and using systems

- Performance—which will always be a research and development topic.

IN CLOSING . . .

The object DBMS market is still relatively immature. The vendors are striving to establish credibility and move their technologies into the mainstream of application development. They face a variety of challenges, which differ somewhat depending on the kind of buyer the vendor is trying to attract. The products based on a "pure" object-oriented approach and tightly integrated with an object programming language tend to appeal to people who are adopting object technology with the expectation of productivity and quality benefits from integrated, synergistic object model support. Other customers are more comfortable building on their legacy of language skills. The object DBMS products that take more of a hybrid approach and offer object extensions to SQL tend to appeal to these people. Time will tell how much room the market will offer to each approach.

REFERENCES

[Agra89]   Agrawal, R., and N. Gehani. ODE (object database and environment): The language and the data model. *Proc. ACM SIGMOD*, Portland, OR, June 1989.

[Alas89]   Alashqur, A., S. Su, and H. Lam. OQL: A query language for manipulating object-oriented databases. *Proc. of the 15th Intl. Conf. on Very Large Databases*, Amsterdam, pp. 433–442, 1989.

[Andr93]   Andrew, T., and D. Krieger. Concurrency control for workgroups. *Object Magazine*, **3**(2):38–45, August 1993.

[ANSI92]   ANSI X3H2. *Database Language SQL*. X3.135–1992.

[ANSI93]   ANSI X3J4.*1/93-0048—Object-Oriented Features Summary* (Version 4), October 1993.

[ANSI94]   ANSI X3H7. *X3H7 Object Model Features Matrix*. Evolving document: ANSI X3H7-93-007.

[Atki78]   Atkinson, M. Programming languages and databases. *Proc. 4th Intl. Conf. on Very Large Databases*. Morgan Kaufmann, pp. 408–419, 1978.

[Atki83]   Atkinson, M., P. Bailey, K. Chisolm, P. Cockshott, and R. Morrison. An approach to persistent programming. *The Computer Journal*, **26**(4):360–365, 1983.

[Atki87]   Atkinson, M., and O. Buneman. Types and persistence in database programming languages. *ACM Computing Surveys*, **19**(2):105–190, 1987.

[Atki89]   Atkinson, M., F. Bancilhon, D. DeWitt, K. Dittrich, D. Maier, and S. Zdonik. The object-oriented database system manifesto. In *Proc. of the Deductive Object-Oriented Database Conference*, Kyoto, Japan, pp. 40–57, December 1989.

[Atre92]   Atre, S. *Distributed Databases, Cooperative Processing and Networking*. New York: McGraw-Hill, 1992.

[Atwo91]   Atwood, T., and J. Orenstein. Notes toward a standard object-oriented DDL and DML. *Computer Standards and Interfaces*. **13**:117–121, 1991.

[Atwo93]   Atwood, T. ODMG-93: The object DBMS standard. *Object Magazine*, **3**(3):37–44, September/October 1993.

[Atwo94]   Atwood, T. ODMG-93: The object DBMS standard, part 2. *Object Magazine*, **3**(5):32ff, January 1994.

[Banc89]   Bancilhon, F., S. Cluet, and C. Delobel. A query language for the O2 object-oriented database system. In Hull, R., R. Morrison, and D. Stemple, eds. *Database Programming Languages. Proc. of the Second Intl. Workshop on Database Programming Languages.* San Mateo, CA: Morgan Kaufmann, 1989.

[Banc90]   Bancilhon, F., and P. Buneman, eds. *Advances in Database Programming Languages.* Reading, MA: Addison-Wesley, 1990.

[Banc94]   Bancilhon, F., and G. Ferran. ODMG-93: The object database standard. O2-Technology, 1994.

[Barr94]   Barry, D. *DBMS Needs Assessment for Objects, Release 2.0.* Minneapolis, MN: Barry & Associates, Inc., 1994.

[Beer89]   Beeri, C., P. Bernstein, and N. Goodman. A model for concurrency in nested transaction systems. *J. of the ACM,* **36**(2):230–269, 1989.

[Beer91]   Beeri, C., and T. Milo. A model for active object-oriented database. In *Proc. of the 17th Intl. Conf. on Very Large Databases.* Morgan Kaufmann, pp. 337–349, 1991.

[Bern81]   Bernstein, P., and N. Goodman. Concurrency control in distributed database systems. *ACM Computing Surveys,* **13**(2):185–221, 1981.

[Bert89]   Bertino, E., and W. Kim. Indexing techniques for queries on nested objects. *IEEE Trans. on Knowledge and Data Engineering,* **1**(2):196–214, 1989.

[Blak91]   Blakeley, J., C. Thompson, and A. Alashgur. A strawman reference model for object query languages. *Computer Standards and Interfaces.* **13**:185–199, 1991.

[Blak94]   Blakeley, J. OQL [C++]; Extending C++ with an object query capability. In Kim, W., ed. *Modern Database Systems: The Object Model, Interoperability, and Beyond.* Reading, MA: ACM Press–Addison-Wesley, 1994.

[Booc91]   Booch, G. *Object-Oriented Design with Applications.* Redwood City, CA: Benjamin/Cummings, 1991.

[Bruc92]   Bruce, T. *Designing Quality Databases with IDEF1X Information Models,* New York, NY: Dorset House Publ., 1992.

[Care88]   Carey, M., D. DeWitt, and S. Vandenberg. A data model and query language for EXODUS. *Proc. of ACM-SIGMOD 1988 Intl. Conf. on Management of Data,* Chicago, IL, pp. 413–423, 1988.

[Care94]   Carey, M., J. DeWitt, and J. Naughton. The 007 benchmark. *SIGMOD Record,* **22**(2):12–21, 1993. Also available as Technical Report No. 1140, Computer Sciences Department, University of Wisconsin—Madison, April 12, 1993, revised January 1994.

[Catt91]   Cattell, R. *Object Data Management: Object-Oriented and Extended Relational Database Systems*. Reading, MA: Addison-Wesley, 1991.

[Catt92]   Cattell, R., and J. Skeen. Object operations benchmark. *ACM Trans. on Database Systems*, **17**(1):1–31, 1992.

[Catt94]   Cattell, R., ed. *The Object Database Standard: ODMG-93, Release 1.1*. San Mateo, CA: Morgan Kaufmann, 1994.

[Cham74]   Chamberlin, D., and R. Boyce. SEQUEL: A structured English query language. *Proc. 1974 ACM SIGMOD Workshop on Data Description, Access, and Control*. May 1974.

[Chen76]   Chen, P. The entity-relationship model—Toward a unified view of data. *ACM Trans. on Database Systems*, **1**(1), March 1976.

[Chen91]   Cheng, J., and A. Hurson. Effective clustering of complex objects in object-oriented databases. *Proc. ACM SIGMOD Intl. Conf. on Management of Data*, pp. 22–31, 1991.

[Codd79]   Codd, E. Extending the database relational model to capture more meaning. *ACM Trans. on Database Systems*, **4**(4), December 1979.

[Cole94]   Coleman, D., P. Arnold, S. Bodoff, C. Dollin, H. Gilchrist, F. Hayes, and P. Jeremaes. *Object-Oriented Development: The Fusion Method*. Englewood Cliffs, NJ: Prentice Hall, 1994.

[Crib92]   Cribbs, J., C. Roe, and S. Moon. *An Evaluation of Object-Oriented Analysis and Design Methodologies*. SIGS Publications, Inc., 1992.

[Date93]   Date, C. A fruitful union. *Computerworld*, p. 130, June 14, 1993.

[Daya89]   Dayal, U. Queries and views in an object-oriented data model. In *Proc. 2nd Intl. Workshop on Database Programming Languages*, pp. 80–102, 1989.

[Daya91]   Dayal, U., M. Hsu, and R. Ladin. A transactional model for long-running activities. In *Proc. 17th Intl. Conf. on Very Large Databases*. San Mateo, CA: Morgan Kaufmann, pp. 113–122, 1991.

[DeAr91]   DeArmon, J. Object-oriented databases: A technology needing a kick start. *D&B Dataquest Research Newsletter*, July 1991.

[Eswa76]   Eswaran, K., J. Gray, R. Lorie, and I. Traiger. The notions of consistency and predicate locks in a data base system. *Communications of the ACM*, **19**(11), November 1976.

[Fish87]   Fishman, D., D. Beech, H. Cate, E. Chow, T. Connors, J. Davis, N. Derrett, C. Hoch, W. Kent, P. Lyngbaek, B. Mahbod, M. Neimat, T. Ryan, and M. Shan. IRIS: An object-oriented database management system. *ACM Transactions on Office Information Systems*, **5**(1):48–69, January 1987.

[Garc91]   Garcia-Molina, H., D. Gawlick, J. Klein, K. Kleissner, and K. Salem. Modeling long-running activities as nested sagas. *Bulletin IEEE Technical Committee on Data Engineering*, **14**(1):14–18, 1991.

[Gart92]   Gartner Group. The strategic impact of object-oriented technology. Presented at the Gartner Group Fifth Annual Applications Development & Managment Strategies Conference, Stamford, CT: Gartner Group, 1992.

[Gray81]   Gray, J. Transaction concepts: Virtues and limitations. *Proc. 7th Intl. Conf. on Very Large Databases*. San Mateo, CA: Morgan Kaufmann, pp. 144–154, 1981.

[Gray91]   Gray, J., ed. *The Benchmark Handbook for Database and Transaction Processing Systems*. San Mateo, CA: Morgan Kaufmann, 1991.

[Gray92]   Gray, J., and A. Reuter. *Transaction Processing: Concepts and Techniques*. San Mateo, CA: Morgan Kaufmann, 1992.

[Gutt84]   Guttman, A. R-trees: A dynamic index structure for spatial searching. *Proc. ACM SIGMOD Intl. Conf. on Management of Data*, Boston, MA, pp. 47–57, June 1984.

[Hamm78]   Hammer, M., and D. McLeod. The semantic data model: A modelling mechanism for data base applications. In *Proc. ACM SIGMOD Intl. Conf. on Management of Data*. Austin, TX, pp. 26–36, May 31–June 2, 1978.

[Harm93]   Harmon, P., and D. Taylor. *Objects in Action: Commercial Applications of Object-Oriented Technologies*. Reading, MA: Addison-Wesley, 1993.

[Hill92]   Hill, N., and S. Woodring. Focus: Sizing the software market. *The Software Strategy Report*, Forrester Research, Inc., May 1992.

[IDC92]   International Data Corp. *Opportunities in Object-Oriented Technologies*. Framingham, MA: International Data Corp., 1992.

[ITG93]   International Techvantage Group. *Expectations and Trends in the Adoption of Object-Oriented Technology*. New York, NY: Techvantage, Inc., 1993.

[Jaco92]   Jacobson, I., M. Christerson, P. Jonsson, and G. Övergaard. *Object-Oriented Software Engineering: A Use Case Driven Approach*. Reading, MA: Addison-Wesley, 1992.

[Jark84]   Jarke, M., and J. Koch. Query optimization in database systems. *ACM Computing Surveys*, **16**(2), June 1984.

[Jeff90]   Jeffcoate, J., and C. Guilfoyle. *Databases for Objects: The Market Opportunity*. London, England: Ovum, Ltd., 1990.

[Khos86]   Khoshafian, S., and G. Copeland. Object identity. In *Proc. Conf. on Object-Oriented Programming Systems and Languages (OOPSLA)*, Portland, OR, September 1986.

[Kort88]   Korth, H., W. Kim, and F. Bancilhon. On long-duration CAD trans-actions. *Information Sciences*, **46**(1–2):73–107, 1988.

[Kung81]   Kung, H., and J. Robinson. On optimistic methods for concurrency control. *ACM Trans. on Database Systems*, **6**(2):213–226, 1981.

[LaLo93]   LaLonde, W., and J. Pugh. Interfacing Smalltalk to relational data-bases. *J. of Object-Oriented Programming*, **5**(6):75–80, September 1993.

[LaLo94]   LaLonde, W., and J. Pugh. ODBMSs and database transparency. *J. of Object-Oriented Programming*, **5**(9):63–67, February 1994.

[Lamb91]   Lamb, C., G. Landis, J. Orenstein, and D. Weinreb. The ObjectStore database system. *Communications of the ACM*, **34**(10), October 1991.

[Loom90a]   Loomis, M. The basics. *J. of Object-Oriented Programming*, **3**(3):77–81, May/June 1990.

[Loom90b]   Loomis, M. ODBMS versus relational. *J. of Object-Oriented Program-ming*, **3**(4):79–82, July/August 1990.

[Loom90c]   Loomis, M. Database transactions. *J. of Object-Oriented Programming*, **3**(4), July/August 1990.

[Loom91a]   Loomis, M. More on transactions. *J. of Object-Oriented Programming*, **3**(8), January 1991.

[Loom91b]   Loomis, M., and K. Rotzell. Benchmarking an ODBMS. *J. of Object-Oriented Programming*, **4**(1):66–72, March/April 1991.

[Loom91c]   Loomis, M. Integrating objects with relational technology. *Object Magazine*, **1**(2):July/August 1991.

[Loom91d]   Loomis, M. Objects and SQL: Accessing relational databases. *Object Magazine*, **1**(3):68–78, September/October 1991.

[Loom92a]   Loomis, M. Object versioning. *J. of Object-Oriented Programming*, **4**(8):40–43, January 1992.

[Loom92b]   Loomis, M. Object database technology: Who's using it and why? *Hotline on Object-Oriented Technology*, pp. 13–18, October 1992.

[Loom92c]   Loomis, M. Application development with objects. *Data Base News-letter*, **20**(6):3–8, November/December 1992.

[Loom93a]   Loomis, M. Object and relational technologies: Can they cooperate? *Object Magazine*, **2**(5):35–40, January/February 1993.

[Loom93b]   Loomis, M. Object programming plus database management. *J. of Object-Oriented Programming*, **5**(9):75–79, February 1993.

[Loom93c]   Loomis, M. Object programming and database management: Differ-ences in perspective. *J. of Object-Oriented Programming*, **6**(2):20–24, May 1993.

[Loom93d]   Loomis, M. The ODMG object model. *J. of Object-Oriented Program-ming*, **6**(3):20–25, June 1993.

[Loom93e]   Loomis, M. Object database semantics. *J. of Object-Oriented Programming*, **6**(4):26ff, July/August 1993.

[Loom93f]   Loomis, M. Managing replicated objects. *J. of Object-Oriented Programming*, **5**(6):65–71, September 1993.

[Loom93g]   Loomis, M. Making objects persistent. *J. of Object-Oriented Programming*, **6**(6):25–28, October 1993.

[Loom94a]   Loomis, M. Hitting the relational wall. *J. of Object-Oriented Programming*, **6**(8):56ff, January 1994.

[Loom94b]   Loomis, M. Querying object databases. *J. of Object-Oriented Programming*, **7**(3):56–60ff, June 1994.

[Loom94c]   Loomis, M. ODBMS myths and realities. *J. of Object-Oriented Programming*, **7**(4):77–80, July/August 1994.

[Love93]   Love, T. *Object Lessons*. SIGS Books, Inc. 1993.

[Maie94]   Maier, D., G. Graefe, L. Shapiro, S. Daniels, T. Keller, and B. Vance. Issues in distributed object assembly. In *Distributed Object Management*, Ozsu, M., ed., San Mateo, CA: Morgan Kaufmann, pp. 165–181, 1994.

[Marg90]   Margaret, A., and B. Stroustrup. *The Annotated C++ Reference Manual*. Reading, MA: Addison-Wesley, 1990.

[Mart92]   Martin, J., and J. Odell. *Object-Oriented Analysis and Design*. Englewood Cliffs, NJ: Prentice Hall, 1992.

[McGo89]   McGoveran, D. Beyond OLTP: On-line complex processing. *InfoDB*, Fall 1989.

[Melt93]   Melton, J., and A. Simon. *Understanding the New SQL: A Complete Guide*. San Mateo, CA: Morgan Kaufmann, 1993.

[Melt94]   Melton, J., ed. *Database Language SQL3*, ISO/ANSI Working Draft, 1994.

[Moor91]   Moore, G. *Crossing the Chasm*. New York, NY: Harper Business, 1991.

[Moss90]   Moss, J. Working with persistent objects: To swizzle or not to swizzle. Computer and Information Science Technical Report 90-38, University of Massachusetts—Amherst, May 1990.

[Obje94]   Objectivity, Inc. SQL and object technology, an objectivity white paper. Menlo Park, CA: 1994.

[OMG92]   Object Management Group, *Object Analysis & Design and Design Survey of Methods 1992*. Technical Report, Object Management Group, Framingham, MA, October 1992.

[Oren91]   Orenstein, J., and E. Bonte. The need for a DML: Why a library interface isn't enough. *Computer Standards and Interfaces*, Vol. 13, pp. 145–150, 1991.

[Ovum89]   Ovum, Ltd. *The Impact of Object-Oriented Systems*. London, England: 1989.

[Ozsu90]   Ozsu, T., and P. Valduriez. *Principles of Distributed Database Systems*. Englewood Cliffs, NJ: Prentice Hall, 1990.

[Pasc93]   Pascal, F. Objection! *Computerworld*, pp. 127–130, June 14, 1993.

[Rumb91]   Rumbaugh, J., M. Blaha, W. Premerlani, F. Eddy, and W. Lorensen. *Object-Oriented Modeling and Design*. Englewood Cliffs, NJ: Prentice Hall, 1991.

[Shaw89]   Shaw, G., and S. Zdonik. An object-oriented query algebra. *Proc. Second Intl. Workshop on Database Programming Languages*, June 1989.

[Ship81]   Shipman, D. The functional data model and the data language DAPLEX. *ACM Trans. on Database Systems*, **2**(3):140–173, March 1981.

[Shla88]   Shlaer, S., and S. Mellor, *Object-Oriented Systems Analysis: Modeling the World in Data*. Englewood Cliffs, NJ: Yourdon Press, 1988.

[Smit77]   Smith, J., and D. Smith. Database abstractions: Aggregation and generalization. *ACM Trans. on Database Systems*. **2**(2):105–133, June 1977.

[Sole92]   Soley, R. M., ed. *Object Management Architecture Guide, Rev. 2, 2nd Ed.* OMG TC Document 92.11.1, Object Management Group, 1992.

[Ston76]   Stonebraker, M., E. Wong, P. Kreps, and G. Held. The design and implementation of INGRES. *ACM Trans. on Database Systems*, **1**(3), September 1976.

[Ston85]   Stonebraker, M., ed. *The INGRES Papers: The Anatomy of a Relational Database Management System*. Reading, MA: Addison-Wesley, 1985.

[Stri92]   Strickland, H. Object databases—A deep look at transparency. C++ *Report*, **4**(5):42–46, 1992.

[Tayl90]   Taylor, D. *Object-Oriented Technology: A Manager's Guide*. Reading, MA: Addison-Wesley, 1990.

[Tayl92]   Taylor, D. *Object-Oriented Information Systems: Planning and Implementation*. New York, NY: Wiley & Sons, 1992.

[Thom93]   Thompson, D. Interfacing objects with the relational DBMS. *Database Programming and Design*, **6**(8):33ff, August 1993.

[Tich94]   Tichy, W., J. Heilig, and F. Paulisch. A generative and generic approach to persistence. C++ *Report*, **5**(10):22–33, January 1994.

[Topp94]   Topper, A. The object-oriented COBOL standard. *Object Magazine*, **3**(6):39–41, February 1994.

[TPC89]   Transaction Performance Council (TPC). *TPC Benchmark: A Standard*. November 1989.

[Tsan92]   Tsangaris, M., and J. Naughton. On the performance of object clustering techniques. *Proc. ACM SIGMOD Intl. Conf. on Management of Data*, pp. 144–153, 1992.

[Vorw94]   Vorwerk, R. Toward a true ODBMS. *Object Magazine*, 3(5):38–39, January 1994.

[Whit92]   White, S., and D. Dewitt. A performance study of alternative object faulting and pointer swizzling strategies. *Proc. 18th Intl. Conf. on Very Large Databases*, Vancouver, British Columbia, Canada, 1992.

[Wirf90]   Wirfs-Brock, R., B. Wilkerson, and L. Wiener. *Designing Object-Oriented Software*. Englewood Cliffs, NJ: Prentice Hall, 1990.

[Wood90]   Woodring, S., and G. Colony. Focus: Object-oriented technology. *The Software Strategy Report*. Cambridge, MA: Forrester Research, Inc., August 1990.

The Journal of Object-Oriented Programming and *Object Magazine* are published by SIGS Publications, Inc., 71 W. 23rd St., Third Floor, New York, NY 10010.

INDEX